ARNOLD PRINCE has been teaching wood and stone sculpture since 1964. In 1972 he became Assistant Professor of Sculpture, Fine Arts Department, Rhode Island School of Design. His work is represented in over 100 private collections, including the Art Students League of New York.

Arnold Prince

CARVING
WOOD AND STONE

an illustrated
manual

PRENTICE-HALL, INC., Englewood Cliffs, N.J. 07632 A SPECTRUM BOOK

Library of Congress Cataloging in Publication Data

PRINCE, ARNOLD, (date)
  Carving wood and stone.

  (A Spectrum Book)
  Includes index.
  1. Wood-carving. 2. Stone carving. I. Title.
TT199.7.P74   731.4'6   80-21530
ISBN 0-13-115311-0
ISNB 0-13-115303-X (pbk.)

To my mother and father

Editorial/production supervision by Carol Smith
Interior Design by Christine Gehring Wolf
Cover Design by Jack Ribik
Manufacturing buyer: Barbara A. Frick

© 1981 by Prentice-Hall, Inc., Englewood Cliffs, New Jersey 07632

A SPECTRUM BOOK

10 9 8 7 6 5 4 3 2 1

Printed in the United States of America

PRENTICE-HALL INTERNATIONAL, INC., *London*
PRENTICE-HALL OF AUSTRALIA PTY. LIMITED, *Sydney*
PRENTICE-HALL OF CANADA, LTD., *Toronto*
PRENTICE-HALL OF INDIA PRIVATE LIMITED, *New Delhi*
PRENTICE-HALL OF JAPAN, INC., *Tokyo*
PRENTICE-HALL OF SOUTHEAST ASIA PTE. LTD., *Singapore*
WHITEHALL BOOKS LIMITED, *Wellington, New Zealand*

contents

foreword

THE opportunity to become involved with a distinctive cultural contribution is rarely offered to anyone. That is one reason why I am delighted beyond words to have been asked by Arnold Prince to write the Foreword to his *Carving Wood and Stone*. He is a sculptor in a true and abiding sense of that art, which he practices and teaches so well. I am also a teacher, though one of literature, but I believe in the cross-fertilization of the arts. Arnold's teaching has led me to a conception of poetry I never knew before, and I acknowledge that his influence has altered the course of my life. Not only have I acquired a new skill, I have also learned to see and to conceptualize in a new and exciting way.

In my case, the transformation—if that is the word to use—came late. In my forty-second year, a good friend, knowing that I enjoyed carving wood, suggested that I join Arnold's evening course in direct carving at the Rhode Island School of Design. I felt intimidated; it was the "I can't do it" syndrome. Then the same friend showed me a sculpture by Arnold that he had just acquired—a massive limestone of a West Indian mother carrying a sick child in the native manner. I was awed by this piece (and still am), and diffidence was erased by a genuine desire to meet the man whose work was so direct and powerful, without a hint of the decadence that seems to permeate most of what passes as art in our society today.

So I took his course and continue to take it—with gusto, may I add. Arnold has a charisma that is hard to pin down. Probably it stems from his West Indian heritage. He is a native of St. Kitts and, in a delightfully spontaneous way, clings to and expresses his cultural heritage, be it in sculpture, music, dance, or speech. And, again, there is no decadence. This man will never be taken in by the meretricious trends and contraptions of the present generation who make disposable art; nor will he ever teach such claptrap.

Arnold was educated in both the Caribbean and America. His undergraduate degree is from the British Public School System in the Caribbean, as monitored by Cambridge University; and in New York, he studied sculpture at the Art Students' League under William Zorach and José de Creeft. His credentials are clearly good.

But his teaching is more than good. To see this spritely man at work, hovering from student to student, is a joy. He knows how to approach and handle each one: what to say and what not to say, when to suggest and when not to, and how to criticize and in what terms. The skill and feeling are enormous, as is the range of his articulation. Sometimes he passes you by with a glance; sometimes he pauses to look and drop a hint; and sometimes he peers deeply before commenting at length. He is always casual, but nonetheless all-knowing.

His students, old and young, love him and thrive on his gentle persuasion and high good spirits. In fact, his book is generously illustrated by their work. But most important is the fact that this book is the first of its kind. Granted, there are scads of volumes on sculpture and sculptors, but this is the first one entirely on *direct* carving. Prior to this book, a chapter here and there has been all we have had; now, the subject is covered step by step and chapter by chapter. As a rule, the pioneer books have a way of holding up, and I believe that this book will do so as well. It deals with all aspects of the great sculptural techniques of the ancient Greeks and of Michelangelo as seen through the eyes of a thoroughly competent contemporary practitioner. The only thing lacking is direct contact with the vital author himself, but the style of the book shows us the man. May the eager student curl up with this book and become a better sculptor for it. No finer introduction to the ancient but recently moribund art of direct carving is available today.

Nathaniel B. Atwater
Department of English
Southeastern Massachusetts University.

preface

DIRECT carving can be described as the art of creating a piece of sculpture from a block of material by the process of removing or subtracting parts of the block in such a way that the unremoved portions of the block express the sculptor's intent. However, this process must include the very special ethic of taking suggestions from the block during the subtraction process.

Although the majority of the sculptures of antiquity were done in wood and stone, the art of direct carving in these materials has become almost lost. It has only recently been reintroduced in the United States, mainly through the efforts of José de Creeft and William Zorach, and in Europe. Now that interest is being rekindled, I find that there are no clear books on how to do it, how to think it. When I was a student at the Art Students League in New York City in the 1950s, I could find only one book on direct carving; written by an Englishman named John Mills, it dealt only with stone. Most other available books are either very general, tending to deal with every aspect of sculpture and often written by people who have never carved, or they are very specific, tending to deal with the life and works of a direct carver, with illustrations of the finished works and no mention at all of the "how" to do it. With this in mind, I have attempted in this book to give the reader insight into this exciting and creative art.

Wood and stone, when carved directly with hand tools, enable the sculptor to use imagination and to seize upon chance after chance as the material changes shape. In this way, a new and creative work is produced that is always a product of the block from which it came and that always bears the sculptor's persuasions.

carving
stone

types of stone best suited for carving
limestone, marble, and alabaster

ALL stones are carvable, but for reasons of hardness or softness I recommend only the medium-hard to soft stones for a beginner in the art of stonecarving. Limestone, alabaster, and marble are best suited for use by the beginner, as well as being excellent for the professional. They are easy to work with and are most readily available, and they also provide a good range of soft to medium to hard stone. This does not mean that other stones not mentioned here are unsuitable for carving, but nothing is missed by the omission of the tough stones except more work, and a sculptor working with these three kinds of stone can develop a good knowledge of stonecarving.

Limestone is the best stone to start with; it is considered to be a good medium-hard stone, not too hard and yet not as soft as the alabasters. All alabasters and all types of marbles are suitable for carving, but I recommend that you begin with limestone. After three limestone carvings, you will have enough confidence to try marble.

The simplest and most direct way to describe marble is to say that marble is limestone in a different form. When heat, pressure, and time combine, deep in the earth, to transform a rock from its original state to a new form, the rock that has been so changed is called *metamorphic rock*. The marbles, in their great varieties, are metamorphic stones transformed from limestone by heat, pressure, time, and chemical actions.

The sculptor's interest in marble differs from that of the geologist. To the sculptor who has worked in limestone, the most important difference between marble and limestone is that marble is harder— much harder than limestone. The next important difference between the two stones is that marble is highly crystallized and glitters under light.

Vermont marbles are softer, and these are recommended as first marbles for the beginner. When the

student gains confidence through carving limestone and soft marbles, then the harder marbles,
such as Georgia and Tennessee marbles, can be
attempted.

Marble is very seldom obtainable in a single color.
More often, even a marble that seems to be gray
will have dark or light streaks suddenly appearing.
Carrara marble from Italy used to be a favorite of
sculptors because it could be depended on to be
a single color, or *unblemished,* the term used then
to describe marble of uniform color. This ethic of
carving uniformly colored stone, particularly white
marble, was popular when the main theme of marble sculpture was the human figure; no sculptor
would risk carving a sculpture of a heroic figure in
white marble only to have a dark gray vein running
from ear to chin and another running horizontally
dead center, cutting the figure in half visually.
Sculpture in marble has since broadened its base:
Its subject matter is universal. Color variations in
marbles are very desirable to contemporary carvers. The sculptor makes the subject suitable to the
marble to be carved, or, if the subject comes first,
the sculptor finds the marble to suit the sculpture.

A form of Tennessee marble is a dark beige and
may be relied on for its uniformity of color. There is
a special beauty to the colorful variations of Vermont marble. White with dark green markings,
white with occasional gold, or dark gray with lighter
gray veins, as well as numerous other color ar-
rangements, are native to Vermont. Deeply colored
veins or markings are often the marks of a separable flaw or fault in the marble. Flaws or faults in
marble do not mean that the stone should not be
carved, only that it has to be carved carefully. Observe the veins and notice if there are cracks. If
cracks appear at the corners, simply break off the
easily separable pieces before starting the sculpture. Remaining flaws that show no cracking can
be carved by making sure to carve across, not
into, the flaws or veins.

Marble is not quarried in every region; however, it is abundant enough to be widely available to the carver. In the western United States, California and Colorado are two regions where marble is quarried. Tennessee, Georgia, and Alabama produce excellent marbles. The Georgia marble is particularly interesting to carve. The crystals are very large, and the marbles are very hard. There is also a bright pink variety of Georgia marble. Georgia marble is also available in white with an occasional dark gray streak.

Although alabaster is related to marble and can even be called a marble, the relationship is purely chemical or technical. In hardness, the two stones are opposite. Alabaster is the softest of stones and is among the most beautiful of carvable stones. Care must be applied because of its soft nature and its composition of faults or veins. The paradox is that the faults and veins are part of its special beauty.

Beginning students of stonecarving should not attempt to carve alabaster until they have worked with medium-hard stones and, better yet, with the marbles. The reason for this is that the extreme softness of alabaster offers no resistance. The lack of resistance tempts the inexperienced sculptor into overcarving and, very often, into producing meaningless, superlatively decorated carvings.

Alabaster has the same fragile beauty as the West Indian coalpot, and it is worth the risk to carve once you have some experience. It is a stone of exquisite beauty. In the past, just as with marble, sculptors sought the most solid color alabasters for carving. The broadening of the range of sculpture has eliminated fastidious tendencies over the choice of stone. There is no reason not to carve a piece of alabaster with many color changes and plenty of flaws. Seeking a flawless piece of alabaster is almost denying the nature of the stone. There are dealers in alabaster who, by a process of selective sorting, can offer flawless alabaster that shows very little color change. But such highly selective alabaster is like all things that deny their own nature—rather boring and lacking in spirit. The exquisite and colorful markings one sees on alabaster are its veins and faults, without which the stone would be bland. Better to carve a real piece of alabaster—with all its character, flaws, and colors. But there is no denying that some persons find the selected uniform alabaster attractive. Italian alabaster is the most reliable if one is seeking the pure white or pink translucent stone. The translucency tends to make the sculpture weightless after it is polished. This can be countered by polishing only parts of the sculpture, leaving tool marks present on most of the work. In this way, the beauty of the alabaster is not denied, and the integrity of the sculpture is allowed. The aim in carving translucent alabaster is to avoid becoming entrapped into creating bonbon baskets of flowers or any such banal decorations. Remain in charge of the sculpture rather than allowing the alabaster to take over.

Additional workable stones are the so-called semiprecious stones. For the sake of simplicity, I shall name the two most available: green serpentine stone and onyx.

Granite, fieldstones, quartz, and basalt are extremely hard and toxic stones. Sandstones are soft but extremely toxic. Although none of these toxic stones are recommended for the beginner, anyone desiring to try them should do so only after making sure to obtain and use a miner's mask or respirator in order to avoid breathing harmful dust.

All stones are dense and heavy. The weight of the material is an important consideration to the carver. Limestones are about 170 pounds per cubic foot, and marbles and alabasters are about 180 pounds per cubic foot.

I have found that a 200-pound block of any stone

is a good minimum weight to start with. Two persons are able to lift this weight and place it on the work table. Also, the measurements of a 200-pound block—slightly over a cubic foot—allow sufficient volume for carving.

sources

The best sources from which to obtain soft stones for carving are cut-stone companies, stonecutters and venders that prepare stones for building purposes. The telephone listing of such companies in the Yellow Pages varies in phrasing; some are listed as "cut stone," others as "stone works"; but it is safe to seek them in the telephone directory under "stone." A good example of such a company is the Adam Ross Company in Albany, New York. There are many more, especially in large cities. From such companies, the sculptor can buy "waste" stones at a reasonable price. "Waste" means fragments left over from cuts made from large blocks for buildings. Some stonework companies will ship stone in bulk as well as small orders.

Another good source for stone is quarries. Cut-stone companies are good information sources for any student of sculpture in stone who wishes to gather information about the location of stone quarries and the availability of any type of stone. It is their business, and I have always been able to rely on them.

Most American limestones are quarried in Indiana, but limestones are available at any cut-stone company that prepares stones for buildings. Many foreign stones are omitted here because the aim is to give a list of the most available stones. However, a large amount of Italian marble is available through most suppliers of stone.

The Vermont Marble Company in Barre and Rutland, Vermont is the main producer and supplier of marble in the eastern United States, and they will ship large or small anywhere, as would most other quarries. In the South, the Georgia Marble Company supplies white and pink Georgia marble—a hard and large-grained stone. The Tennessee Marble Company quarries a hard beige marble.

The marble quarries are not the best sources from which to obtain marble, if all that is required are a few small pieces of 200 pounds or less. Of course, if you live within a comfortable drive from a quarry, then a trip to the yard where wastes or fragments are kept can be rewarding.

Better sources of scraps of marble with which to practice carving are the cut-stone companies or tombstone makers nearest you. Stonecutters who design tombstones tend to work mostly in granite, but they very often keep onyx, marble, and other ornate stones in stock for use in special effects.

Building demolition sites are high on the list for carvable marbles. Bear in mind that marbles found at an old building have been exposed to the weather for a long time and, as a result, are much harder than freshly quarried stone.

When José de Creeft introduced direct carving in stone at the Art Students' League in the late 1950s, six of us students went to a section of New York City called "Hell's Kitchen," which was being demolished to make way for the Lincoln Center for the Performing Arts. From the rubble of the demolished "Hell's Kitchen," we gathered two years' supply of excellent marble for the entire class. Later on, we learned that the weathered stones were quite hard; but since it was free, the compensation was free trial by error. From then on, most of the stones for the carving class at the League were obtained from the site of razed buildings.

Alabaster is not produced in as many places as marble; it is a rare stone. Most alabaster obtainable in the United States at art supply stores is the imported and selected Italian variety. My own preference is a domestic alabaster called Colorado alabaster, a good carvable stone of great beauty. This is an opaque stone, buff to off-white, with beautiful black, gold, green, and salmon veining. Its opaque nature spares me the need to counter the translucence of the other types. Colorado alabaster is available in boulders of about 200 pounds and over from the Colorado Alabaster Supply, 1507 North College Avenue, Fort Collins, Colorado 80524. The company will ship a listing catalogue as well as fill orders for alabaster boulders or blocks.

The student or professional sculptor wishing to work with any stone that has to be shipped can make it more feasible to encourage supply companies to ship by teaming up with others in order to increase the volume of the stones ordered, especially if the supply companies have a minimum weight attached to orders. Teaming up with other sculptors for the purpose of obtaining stones for carving is a very productive idea. Sculptors tend to work in groups because of this need; as a result, there is quite a lot of sharing of ideas.

2

stonecarving tools

AMONG the reasons that promoted the decline in the practice of direct carving, two of the foremost causes were the prevalent use of the pointing machine and the advent and use of pneumatic power tools on stone. Later, pneumatic power tools were adapted for use on wood.

The pointing machine can be likened to a pantograph or copying device. The pointing machine system of stonecarving requires that the sculpture to be wrought in stone must first be produced as a model in clay. The sculptor's clay model is then delivered to the pointing machine technician, who proceeds to copy in stone (with the pointing machine) what the sculptor made in clay, usually increasing the scale. This method of sculpture was thought to be stonecarving, but it actually forced the stone to imitate clay and clay concepts.

The copying method—from clay to stone—requires a most laborious process of measuring every projection and depression on the clay model, as well as every angle of the forms, in order to transfer these to the stone. For example, if the distance between the tip of a nose and its base is 1 inch in depth and 45° in slant, then the pointing machine technician sinks a hole into the stone, using the same depth and angle of the model, at the location where the nose is to appear. The excess stone is then removed down to the depth of the hole. In this way, the clay model is duplicated in the stone. Hundreds and sometimes thousands of holes are bored in this process of forcing a block of stone to conform to the plastic clay, until at last a lifeless stone sculpture is produced—one that is both derivative of its clay parent and stifled to death by it. Totally missed in this clay-to-stone system is that direct carving, unharnessed by a clay model, is a creative process that gets its vitality and life from the block of material from which it has been released.

Although there is evidence that the ancient Greek sculptors had knowledge of some type of pointing machine copy device, it was not widely used until during, and especially after, the Renaissance.

Sometimes it is easy to see that a specific stone sculpture is derivative of a clay model; full proof of this is often left by the pointing machine operator, who sometimes bores the holes too deeply, so that the finished sculpture may have holes left in some places. Some of Rodin's stone pieces contain some of these holes and provide clear evidence that the great French sculptor's stone pieces were entrapped by the pointing machine.

The pneumatic or power-driven chisels enable the user to impose heavily upon the block of material to be carved. This process of carving by power tools produces a "power-tool sculpture." Again, sculptors thought to lessen the labor by process of an invention. However, the power tool sculptures are lacking in sensitivity when compared to those that are carved directly using hand-driven chisels, for the resistance of the materials—wood or stone—provides a great deal of the charm of the finished work. Power-driven tools remove this needed resistance. The results of this type of carving are nearly always fussy, overwrought, and lifeless. Viewing power-tool carvings leaves one with the uncomfortable feeling that the stone or wood has been slaughtered.

It is when you carve directly with hand tools that you can truly experience the exhilaration of creating. The all-important first step is to become familiar with the tools. Some of the most common ones are pictured in Figure 2–1. Once you have learned to use the tools, you can let your imagination take flight as a block of stone evolves into a sculpture.

The pitching tool is also called the bull-pointing tool, and pitching a piece of stone is called *bull pointing*. The pitching tool is a heavy chisel that is designed to break off fairly large pieces of stone

how to use the tools
the pitching tool

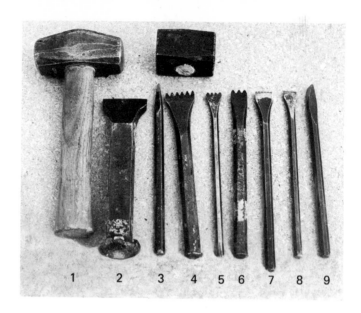

FIGURE 2–1 Stonecarving Tools. 1. The 2-pound stonemason's or sculptor's sledge. 2. The pitching tool. 3. Medium point. 4. Six-tooth claw chisel. 5. Four-tooth claw chisel. 6. Three-tooth claw chisel. 7. Flat-tooth finishing chisel. 8. ¾-inch toothless finishing chisel. 9. ½-inch toothless finishing chisel. Unnumbered is a student's hammerhead with square ends, designed to minimize missing. (Photo by the author)

after a series of heavy blows. It functions by fracturing the stone. The pitching method works only at the corners and edges of the block. Its use is important only to break up the rigid outlines of the cube. the shape in which most blocks of stone are obtained from the stonecutters or stone suppliers.

The pitching tool is particularly helpful if the sculptor depends on the accidental breaking off of pieces of stone to leave suggestions of an image seeming to emerge from the block. Many sculptors depend on this preliminary pitching to start ideas for a particular sculpture. a spontaneous and unplanned sculpture. It is similar to the use of imagination in discerning recognizable forms in clouds as they move across the sky, changing shape according to the wind.

The cutting edge of the pitching tool has one side recessed; the advanced edge is the edge to be placed against the stone when pitching (see Figure 2–2). To pitch large pieces of stone in the preliminary blocking of a sculpture, place the advanced edge of the pitching tool against the block—preferably at the top and about two inches, at most, from the edge. Grasp the tool firmly and strike hard with the hammer. By moving the tool to the left and right, the stone is "scored," and after a short time, a fairly large piece will fall off. With a little practice, the user soon realizes that the pitching tool must be used with restraint and good judgment, for it can reduce the block of stone to total fragments. Never pitch inward toward the masses of the block; always pitch outward toward the edge—toward space (see Figure 2–3).

The sculptor's hammer is also known, in hardware store language, as a stonemason's 2-pound sledge. Two pounds is the best weight hammer for **the hammer or stonemason's sledge**

FIGURE 2–3 Always pitch outward toward the edge of the stone. (Photo by Nick Prinz)

FIGURE 2–2 Place the pitching tool near a corner or edge of the stone so that the bend or bevel faces outward. The arrow in the figure points to the bend. (Photo by Gil McMillon)

the stonecarver's use. Too light a hammer causes the user to swing mightily, tiring the arm, and miss. A hammer heavier than 2 pounds is too weighty for general use; it jars the arm and hand. In using the 2-pound hammer, the weight and balance of the hammer are exploited by raising the forearm and allowing the hammer's weight to fall with a downward motion. The handle provided with the hammer is usually too long. I have found that by removing 2 inches from the end, leaving roughly a 6-inch-long handle, the balance of the hammer improves greatly.

The stonemason's sledge is rounded at the striking ends. This rounding of the hammer ends poses problems for the beginner; it can be a reason for missing. To minimize missing, sculpture supply stores have a variety of what are called students' hammers. These hammers vary in weight from 1 to 2 pounds but have a square hitting end, measuring 1¾ inches square on the 2-pound hammer and 1¼ inches square on the lighter student's hammer. The student's hammer is recommended for persons who continually miss the chisel head and strike their fingers.

In using the hammer, the action varies according to intent. For finishing work with chisels, rapid and light tapping with a steady arm and a flexing wrist is best. For heavy work with the pitching tool or the point, the arm must be swung in order to bring the weight of the hammer into play.

the point and chisels The point is the most important chisel used in stonecarving. It is possible to execute a piece of sculpture in stone using only the point and to consider it finished without having to apply any other tools to the piece. The importance of dexterity with the point cannot be overstressed. The point is the "roughing out" or blocking tool, the tool that describes the artist's intentions through the forms it creates.

If it is possible to figure the angle, the point should be held at about a 45° angle to the stone's surface. Hold the point loosely in the fist and tap the point firmly with the 2-pound hammer. This action causes the point to create a groove as it travels across the surface of the stone. It is necessary to change the angle of the point slightly as the groove moves away from the starting point, sometimes tilting the point backward toward yourself and sometimes tilting it forward to the original 45° angle (see Figure 2–4).

After you have made a series of grooves about 1 inch apart, made by making new incisions between existing grooves, the stone will pop out to the depth of the grooves. In this way, the sculptor, with the use of the point, influences the block of stone to yield forms.

When hammering, the stonecarver never looks at the head of the point where the hammer makes its

FIGURE 2–4 Hold the point at about a 45° angle to the stone and tap firmly with the 2-pound hammer. (Photo by Nick Prinz)

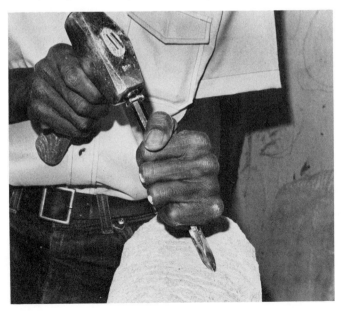

impact. Instead, one must look at the tip of the tool where it makes contact with the stone. Looking at the head of the point while striking with the hammer causes hypnosis, which may cause the sculptor to miss and then to hit his or her fingers, inflicting painful and inhibiting damage.

While I was a student at the Art Students' League of New York, one of my classmates continually missed the point. We were all very concerned about the condition of her left thumb, which bore the brunt of all her misses. Each morning we would bandage her thumb and pad it with sponges in anticipation of more hammer blows. This became a ritual, until someone discovered that she looked fixedly at the point of impact between hammer and point instead of at the cutting edge of the tool. With that simple discovery, we were able to remove the bandages and pads, and she was on her way to carving stone.

An interesting feature in the practice of carving is that one must depend upon the "other hand" to do all of the sensitive work. A right-handed person must hold the point in the left hand and the hammer in the right; the opposite is true if one is left-handed.

To start that first cut, place the tip of the point against the block of stone, preferably on the top side and near the edge; angle the point at about 45°, holding it loosely, and then tap the point firmly with the hammer and guide the point as it travels into its groove. Tap with the hammer to the rhythm of a slow one, two, three, then stop and look. A groove is made in the stone, and some chips fly out: You are now discovering that stone is not tough but that, in order to be an artist with stone, restraint must be applied. After a series of grooves have been made, and after you have made grooves between those grooves, as described above, you may use cross-hatching. As the name suggests, cross-hatching means making new grooves that are not parallel to but at an angle with existing grooves. This technique hastens the subtraction process and creates an interesting texture on the surface of the stone (see Figure 2–5).

The scorings or grooves made by the point must be shallow at the start and definitely deeper at the finish of the stroke. If the depth of the point grooves is the same throughout, the beginner is working too timidly. If the student carves point grooves of the same depth throughout, then the stone will be reduced in volume without changing shape. Beginners' inhibitions about carving are a natural first reaction to the breaking of something, a reaction that has to be overcome. The paradox of direct carving is that through subtraction, both volume and the expansion of forms are gained. The whole truth about direct carving is that it is an art of subtraction. Nothing subtracted means nothing projected; nothing ventured, nothing gained.

FIGURE 2–5 Pointing a piece of limestone—a good example of cross-hatched point grooves. (Photo by Gil McMillon, Rhode Island School of Design)

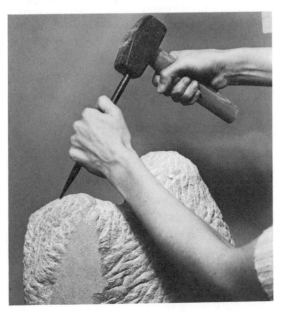

In direct carving, if one desires to execute a protrusion into space of, say, 6 inches, it can only be done by a subtraction from the surface inward to a depth equal to the protrusion desired.

If, through timidity, the beginner uses the point with insufficient aggression, a large boulder will become a small boulder, or a large square block will become a smaller square block. The aim should be to change the original shape of the material and slowly to coax it into assuming new forms according to the sculptor's will. I knew a sculptor on the East Side in New York City in the late 1950s who made beautiful miniature sculptures in stone. His finished pieces weighed about 20 pounds. One day, I went to his studio and was surprised to see him working on a block of stone at least 300 pounds in weight. I asked him if he was doing a large piece this time. He said no, that he always started with a 300-pound block in order to get a 20-pound piece of sculpture! As I watched him work, I realized that he simply went round and round with the point, as if peeling a potato, afraid to move in, until at last, just before the block totally disappeared into chips, he'd be forced to make decisions and make a sculpture out of the largest remaining chip.

To avoid acquiring early bad habits, the students of carving should make sure that point grooves are deeper at the finish of the groove as the point advances from the starting position.

the claw or tooth chisels

The claw or tooth chisels, designed for carving stone, are simple in shape. These claw chisels are very efficient and can become, in a sculptor's hand, tools as intimate as painter's brushes.

The claw chisels refine and clarify the forms roughed out by the point. Claw chisels vary in width and also in the number of teeth each has: from two teeth upward to eight or more, and from ¼ inch to 2 inches or more in width. I have found that the most practical chisel has three to six teeth and varies from ½ inch in width up to 1¼ inches.

The claw chisel has pointed and widely spaced teeth, but the finishing claw chisel has teeth that are flattened and closely spaced. There are also finishing chisels that are toothless. These are called flat chisels and are not unlike a carpenter's flat chisel, except that they are tempered for use on stone. A good range of flat finishing chisels is from ½ inch in width up to 1¼ inches. The wider the chisel, the broader the area it sweeps. For close work, one needs narrow chisels. In using the claw chisel, grasp it firmly in the left hand—that is, if the user is right-handed. Hold the chisel low on the handle, almost at the point where the handle joins the chisel. Press the chisel hard against the stone, using the heel of the palm to apply the pressure. If the pressure is right, the beginner should get a nice callus on the palm. With the chisel pressed firmly against the stone, tap the handle rapidly with the hammer. Watch and guide the chisel as it travels across the forms, using it to shape the sculpture according to your plans—in much the same way that a painter imposes wishes through the paintbrush.

The chisel must never be driven toward the user; it should travel up, down, left, or right. Regardless of the type of stone you are carving, the claw chisel should be used in every direction except toward the user. Avoid using the chisel in a single direction; move it around in order to feel the forms in every direction.

Although the claw chisel does remove quantities of stone, it would be best if the user does not consider it to be just a tool to remove excess stone. Preferably, think of the claw chisel as a refiner of the forms. One can actually feel the forms through the chisels, as in Figure 2–6. Feel the forms up and over the hills, down into the planes, and into the valleys of the stone; then, tilting the chisel to one

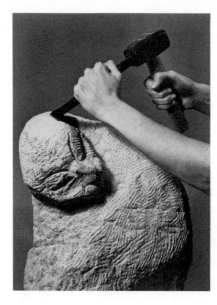

FIGURE 2-6 Feeling the forms with the claw chisel. (Photo by Gil McMillon, Rhode Island School of Design)

side, one can tilt the planes, stopping in a recess that becomes a shadow. That's the kind of intimacy that comes with enough practice with the claw chisels.

where to get tools   If there is a blacksmith in your area, you can have your tools made to order, for the art of forging and tempering stonecarving tools is the blacksmith's art. Many sculptors have learned to forge steel in order to fashion their own tools, but they soon discover that the time consumed and the equipment involved in forging and tempering stonecarving tools make it more expedient to purchase the tools from a supplier.

Most stone quarries sell stonecarving tools, and many of them have stone-tool catalogues and will mail orders. When ordering stonecarving tools care should be taken to obtain hand-held and hammer-driven tools, because stone quarries also stock the power-driven tools, which are unsuitable for hand carving. When ordering stone tools, be sure to specify which type you want—"for hand use." The tools designed for use in pneumatic-driven machines are longer than the hand-held tools.

Sculpture supply stores exist in major cities. College book shops are good sources for obtaining stonecarving tool suppliers.

Craft or art supply stores either sell stonecarving tools or can order them upon request. Woodcarving tools are more readily obtainable at art supply stores than are stonecarving tools.

Two good suppliers of wood and stonecarving tools are: Sculpture Associates, 114 East 25th Street, New York, New York 10010 and Woodcraft Supply Corp., 313 Montrale Avenue, Woburn, Massachusetts 01888. Both companies issue illustrated catalogues of the tools they sell and will ship orders anywhere, large as well as small.

The points used in stonecarving are forged and tempered by the manufacturers so that they are sold ready for use. No sharpening is needed until after they have been used.

how to sharpen stone tools
points

For our purposes here, it can be simply stated that tempering of the metal means hardening the metal. In stonecarving points and chisels, only the cutting tips—about ½-inch—of the tools are tempered; the remainder of the tool is left soft (see Figure 2–7). For example, a point is about 7½ inches long. Seven inches are soft, bendable metal, and the ½ inch at the tip is a tough, uncompromising cutting tip. The tools will work only if they have a soft body and a hard-tempered tip. If the entire length of a point were tempered hard, as you held it into the stone, the tool would bounce mightily when struck with the hammer. If it were totally tempered, it would also vibrate and hurt the hand. Good sharpening habits are important in order to protect the precious tempered tip, for after use and grinding

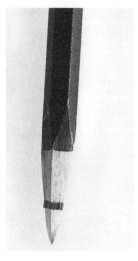

FIGURE 2–7 Only the tip of the stonecarving point is tempered hard; the rest of the tool is soft. Tape marks approximate the tempered portion. (Photo by Gordon Cruz)

have worn away the ½-inch tip, all of the remaining metal is useless for cutting stone unless it is reforged and retempered. Keep all of your worn out tools; you may run into a blacksmith.

If the point tip bends when applied to the stone, that is the signal that all of the tempered tip has been sharpened away or, in some cases, that the temper has simply been lost from being heated while sharpening. A tempered tip will not bend. The cutting tip of a stonecarving point can become useless in one hour if it becomes too hot during sharpening. Heat is the agent that produced the temper, and heat is also capable of removing the temper.

Sharpening the tools upon a turning wheel produces heat, which must be controlled by keeping the sharpened tool wet. Constantly dip the tool in water while sharpening it. The hand-driven sharpening stone is a grinding wheel, usually of carborundum stone, with a handle that enables the user to rotate the wheel and regulate its speed. The electric-powered sharpening wheel is merely the hand-cranked type with an electrically powered motor. The electric type has a fixed speed, but it leaves both of the user's hands free to regulate the angle at which the tool is held against the wheel.

Whether the sharpening wheel is hand-driven or electric-powered, the wheel should turn toward the user when sharpening. The movement of the wheel toward the user facilitates sharpening quickly and efficiently. Wheels that turn away from the user scrape the tools and wear away metal without making the edge keen. Sharpening with the turning wheel requires special care to hold the tool at the proper angle to the wheel. Some wheels have guidebars that can be set to ensure that the angle is constant. Practice sharpening with and without the guidebar. My preference is to sharpen without the guide. The advantage is that the tool is not fixed, which permits constant adjustments to visual observations and needs as the sharpening progresses. Working without the guide requires a steady hand. To sharpen the point, first make the following observations. Most points have seven-sided handles, changing to four sides toward the end and, finally, to a round, tapering tip. The four sides just before the tip aid in the sharpening by providing four flat planes to be placed against the wheel. Keep rotating the point as the grinding wheel turns. Use your eye and your judgment to determine when the point is sharp. Dip the point in water frequently. Maintain the original gentle slope toward the tip.

After sharpening, the tip can be honed with a hand-held whetting stone. Extremely fine files are excellent for finishing the sharpening process.

There are no rules about the best way to use hand-held sharpening stones. Some people prefer to fix the tool in a bench vise and move the stone against the blade. Others prefer to place the whetting stone on the work table and rotate or push the edge of the tool against it. The use of a hand-held whetting stone after sharpening on the grinding wheel is not absolutely necessary, although the practice helps to refine the edge. A newly sharpened point should be used gently for the first few minutes to give the newly heated tip time to set.

Sometimes if a newly sharpened tip is subjected to immediate drastic use, it may break off.

chisels The flat finishing chisels and the claw or tooth chisels require less frequent sharpening than the points. Their use does not bring them into drastic contact with the stone. Chisels are tempered in the same manner as the points: They have soft handles or bodies and hard-tempered cutting edges. Claw-tooth chisels are beveled on both sides toward the end of the tool. Some flat chisels are beveled on one side, and some are not beveled at all. When sharpening beveled chisels, maintain the line of the bevel (see Figure 2–8). Place the chisel against the grinding wheel at an angle that brings, first, the bevel and then the cutting edge into contact with the wheel. Do not produce a second bevel. If this should happen, keep grinding until one true pitch is obtained from bevel to cutting edge. Keep the tool wet and place alternate sides of the chisel to the wheel for even sharpening. After sharpening the chisel on the wheel, a small three-sided file can be used to sharpen between the teeth. The chisel can then be honed with a sharpening stone.

Flat chisels that are beveled on one side only require that the beveled side be sharpened first. When sharpening flat chisels with no bevel, simply maintain the gentle slope from shank to blade.

FIGURE 2–8 When sharpening a beveled chisel, maintain the line of the bevel. The black line is slightly above the bevel, or pitch. (Photo by Gordon Cruz)

Sharpening the pitching tool requires the same observations as with the beveled flat chisel. One side of the pitching tool is beveled. The cutting edge advances from the bevel. When sharpening, maintain the angle between the bevel and the edge. After the tool has been well used, it is sometimes necessary to grind the bevel back into fresh metal so that the bevel and the edge are not on the same line. When the pitching tool is held at a 90° angle to a flat surface, only the advanced edge—not the bevel—should touch the surface.

A great part of sharpening tools properly will come with practice. There are no rules; as long as what you do works, then do it. I use all sides of the sharpening wheel—the left side, the right side, and the edge—even though the manufacturers probably intended the edge of the wheel to be the portion used for sharpening.

3

**how to carve
a piece
of stone**

the carving process
working with stone

THE tools I use are a medium point, backed up with a slender point for close work; two claw chisels with three and five teeth; and a pitching tool, just in case I may find it feasible to speed up the breaking up of the cubelike shape of the block. A 2-pound hammer completes the tool list. However, an important addition is some kind of eye protection against flying stone chips. Eye protectors can be goggles or a transparent face mask. Some sculptors prefer the mask because, with goggles, stone chips strike the face at a high rate of speed during carving. Others prefer goggles because the transparent face mask does not allow enough fresh air to reach the user. The ideal face and eye protector is a combination of goggles and mask (see Figure 3–1). Use goggles and a mask when pointing heavily, and wear goggles only when using the claw chisels. I have not included any finishing tools at this beginning stage, for the presence of finishing tools at the early stage of a sculpture encourages their premature use.

Small stones should be raised from ground level for easy reach during the carving process. Also, dur-

FIGURE 3–1 Use a face mask and/or protective goggles when carving stone or wood. (Photo by Gordon Cruz)

ing the carving process, the sculpture is best viewed at eye level, with the sculptor standing. A sturdy table is needed for this purpose. Tables built to serve as furniture are nearly always too fragile; or if they are strongly built for such a purpose, they are likely to have a massive top—a top so large that when you walk to the other side, the stone is out of reach. A good table can be built with pine or fir legs, 4" x 4", to a height of about 2½ feet, also of pine or fir. The top need not exceed 2 feet square (see Figure 3–2).

One of the advantages of starting to discover stone carving with a stone not exceeding 200 pounds is that two or three persons can lift such a weight onto a table without the aid of hoists, and after the sculpture is completed, the sculptor can handle it alone. Large and heavy stones should be avoided at the beginning but should be tackled as confidence and proficiency develop. Hydraulic jacks and overhead chain-fall hoists are some of the systems used by sculptors to lift heavy stones up onto sturdy tables prior to carving. However, if the stu-

FIGURE 3–2 A sturdy table suitable for carving wood or stone. Note the 4″ × 4″ legs. (Photo by Chee Heng Yeong)

dent limits the weight of the stone to 200–300 pounds, such equipment would be unnecessary. Should a stone exceed 300 pounds, it is best carved on the ground or floor. The beginning stonecarver should avoid extra heavy blocks and take comfort in the fact that the size of the sculpture does not necessarily dictate the quality of the work.

Sculptors are constantly presented with the problem of having to lift and move heavy materials. Some sculptors avoid the problems caused by heavy weights by working on a small scale. The more adventurous work on a large scale and use lifts and hoists to cope with the weight of the materials.

The capacity load that a floor can safely hold is also important in determining the weight of stone or wood that one can work with. Even more important in determining the scale of the sculptor's work is the floor level of the studio (ground level, second floor, etc.); if the studio is not on the ground level, then the presence or absence of an elevator is crucial. The capacity of the elevator is also decisive in influencing the scale of a work.

The best space for a carver in wood and stone is on ground level. If there is a basement below, find out the number of pounds per square foot that the floor will tolerate. Local fire departments are equipped to make such determinations.

The best general purpose lift that I have discovered and that has proved to be useful to the carver is a Presto lift (see Figure 3–3). Presto lifts are manufactured to carry various load capacities. I have found a lift capable of raising 1,000 pounds to be adequate, because stones or wood above that weight need not be placed on a work table but are best worked on the ground. Presto lifts are manufactured by various engineering companies. To lo-

FIGURE 3–3 A Presto lift. This lift can raise 1,000 lbs. (Photo by Gil McMillon)

cate one, consult "engineering" in your phone directory and call until you locate one.

In Figure 3–3, the forks of the lift are half raised. A pedal pumped by foot raises the forks, and another pedal, when depressed, lowers the forks to about 1 inch from the ground. Because the forks can be lowered to almost ground level, it is easy to pry the load up and slip the forks under. The Presto lifts are hydraulic in action.

Although chain hoists (chain falls) are excellent for lifting heavy loads, they cannot be recommended for use by the beginner—or even to most practicing sculptors—because chain hoists require firm and elaborate overhead mounts from which they can be hung and safely used. The erection of such mounts is not a common feasibility.

A simple two-wheel hand cart is the ideal weight trucker for the sculptor (see Figure 3–4). This simple and commonly available cart can pick up a load from ground level because the metal ramp rests on the ground and merges with it, much like a dust pan. Two persons are usually needed to load a two-wheel cart, especially if the weight being loaded exceeds 100 pounds. The two-wheel hand cart is a studio must for the carver. They are available at hardware stores.

sources of ideas   What to carve is often a problem for the beginner. The following is an account by Ann Jon, a stone-carver, on how she discovers her subject matter and her approach to carving.

One day I realized that my previous sculptures needed more substance in the subject matter, as well as in the context of the philosophy of the work. With this realiza-

FIGURE 3–4 A two-wheel hand cart. The ramp which extends to the front lies flush with the ground, making it easy to load heavy weights. (Photo by Gil McMillon)

tion, I rejected stonecarving chisels and stone, wood-carving gouges and wood. I returned to clay.

I wanted to work with the clay in the freest way possible; I kept the pieces on a small scale (about 12 inches high) using no wire support for the clay and no tools except my hands and a wooden board to firm up whatever shapes may appear as I pushed the clay around. Many new forms and ideas happened during this process. Most of these ideas were discarded as unsuitable for new directions; but some were kept and developed until they were ready to be transferred from the perishable clay to more permanent plaster, using the "waste mold" process for the transfer of the sculpture from clay to plaster.

Finally I had ten new figures and other forms, which I assembled into one. This new sculptural idea was composed of bricks, female figures, a minotaur, and horn symbols. The last of the female figures became the maquette or model for my next carving.

Simultaneous with developing new forms, I conceived a new context for them. Working my way backward through history, from Greek to Cretan to Sumerian civilization, I found in the myths and poetry of the goddess Inanna such rich and stimulating materials for my imagination that this mythology became the center of my ongoing work. I had become impatient with the small scale of the first models, and looking around my studio I rediscovered a six-foot-tall limestone. Setting the limestone up on one end, I began to carve it, using the maquette in Figure 3–5 as a guide (see also Figure 3–6). I followed the maquette very closely, lest I should wander off my present attempt at new directions, and repeat the old forms which I was now trying to avoid. As I worked in the large stone, I became freer and more in harmony with the newly found forms in this larger scale and in harder material than the clay. Recall that the experiments for new ideas were done in clay. Suddenly, as I worked on the stone, I had a thought to paint on its surface with oil paints (see Figure 3–7). This I did, first as guidelines from which to cut, then for expression to heighten the visual experience, and finally in free patterns to prevent myself, the stone, and the sculpture from becoming too static.

It is amazing how colors can lighten your mind and hand as you work on stone. I also experimented with

FIGURE 3–5 Sculpture by Ann Jon. "The last of the female figures became the maquette or model for my next carving." (Photo by the artist)

FIGURE 3–6 "I had become impatient with the small scale of the first models, and looking around my studio I rediscovered a six-foot-tall limestone." (Photo by the artist)

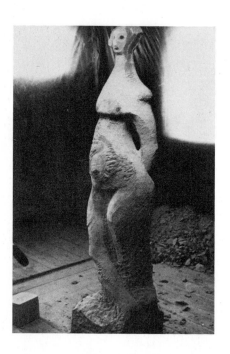

FIGURE 3–7 The use of paints on the stone surface can be seen on the head, eyes, and mouth. (Photo by the artist)

leaving parts of the vanishing forms unremoved from the sculpture. The vanishing forms are the portions of materials that must be carved away and off as the sculpture develops, in much the same way that the outer layers of a nut are peeled away and discarded as one searches for the kernel of the nut. By leaving this bypassed or discarded stone unremoved, I realized that the sculpture acquired a dimension of time and place for the viewers' imagination.

I wanted to express through my sculpture, both feelings of timelessness and of universal time, the former being that suspended state of happiness when everything is given and the latter being the freedom to step out of your time and place and into unexplored experiences. I wanted to combine contemporary sculptural forms with past spiritual concepts, and to express human response to worldly and numinous experiences (see Figures 3–8 and 3–9).

FIGURE 3–8 Front view of the finished piece shows the carved forms and the painted designs working in harmony. (Photo by the artist)

FIGURE 3–9 Back view of the finished sculpture hewn from a 6-foot-high block of limestone. The lively and voluptuous shapes seen in the front view are continued in the back. The dark smudges are painted accents. (Photo by the artist)

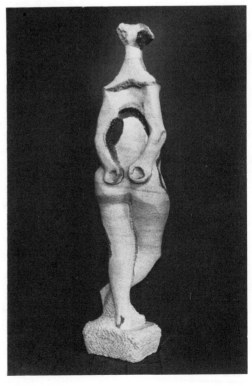

high point and low point; positive and negative spaces

The expression *high point* is a term used especially by sculptors who carve directly; the term refers to those points on a form that are highest in elevation or that thrust out most into space. For example, on a head, it is most likely that the tip of the nose is the highest high point of the planes of the face; the next highest point may be the brows, or perhaps the lips, these things being dictated by the features. Recognizing the highest points on a plane is important to the carver because, in the art of direct carving, the sculptor proceeds from the points of highest elevation inward to points of lower and lowest levels. These elevations and depressions between levels of planes are called positive and negative forms and spaces. It can be said that direct carving depends upon an interplay between the positive forms and the negative spaces or passages between them. In fact, the success of the sculpture depends upon an understanding of these.

A positive form in a sculpture is a solid, unbroken mass that usually projects outward into space. Two such positive forms create a negative space or spaces between them. Let's refer to hills and valleys and apply these terms to carving. Two mountain peaks adjacent to each other, thrusting upward into space, can be called positive forms, and the space between these mountains can be called the negative space. If these forms—mountains and valleys—were to be treated as a direct carving from a block, one would certainly have to deal with the mountain peaks and the mountains before reaching down into, or dealing with, the valley. Why? Because the peaks are the high points and are encountered at the most external surface of the block. The pitfall encountered by most beginners in dealing with the above problem is the tendency to deal with the valley or negative space right from the start—that is, to mistakenly carve the space before carving the objects that create the space. In many forms of visual arts, the artist may be able to work into the negative space prior to discovering the positive forms or masses; however, in direct carving, this practice is denied because of the nature of the act of carving. A premature rendering of the negative spaces in a carving will result in the failure of the piece.

A good example of the proper handling of positive and negative forms in the early stages of a carving of a head would be to make a cut from the tip of the nose (highest point) to the base of the neck (low point) without the least attempt to define or undercut the base of the nose, the lips, or the chin. The reason that this "no definition" of the negatives is so crucial to the success of the sculpture is that the positive forms—nose, mouth, chin, and neck—must relate to each other. Early separation of the positive forms causes them to move apart as the sculpture develops because, in a carving, the forms shift and change as more and more pieces of material are graded off with the chisels.

carving a head in limestone

The stone selected for this carving venture is a piece of limestone 34 inches high, 10 inches broad, and 8 inches in depth. I have chosen to carve a head for this demonstration because the stone is elongated and will allow me to carve a head with a graceful neck—and perhaps a hand. A sculpture of the human head is a good common ground on which to meet because it is a shape that we see frequently and also because it is a shape that we look at with special perception.

As shown in Figure 3–10, I have decided to tackle the flat top of the stone with the pitching tool. The aim is to round the top and change the cubelike shape of the stone. Care will be taken to use this tool only at the top and the corners. It is a fracturing tool, and this is a slender block with no extra volume. In the photograph, a large fragment can

FIGURE 3–10 A large fragment can be seen about to slide off at the third strike of the hammer on the pitching tool. (Photo by Gil McMillon)

be seen about to slide off at the third stroke of the pitcher. The breaking off of fragments leaves shapes that begin to suggest specific forms—a good aid if the sculptor has no specific subject in mind. My first concern is to establish the main high point. The arrow points to one corner of the stone—the corner I have chosen to establish the high points of the head. This high point runs centrally through the top of the head, the center of the forehead, the nose, the mouth, and the center of the chin and throat. The same high point runs centrally through the back of the head and the back of the neck. Identification of the high points on any form is not a system of carving, but it is a recognition of the basic design of the forms to be carved—an understanding that the carver must have. Because the block to be carved presents only the outermost points, the carver must seek the interior forms by moving inward, marking the high points as a guide from which to carve inward.

When a head is seen in side view, the outline of the profile describes the highest points and their relationships to each other. By placing the high point profile at a corner of the stone, I have taken advantage of the "V" shape of the corner, from which the stone thrusts sharply inward in the same way that the planes of the head move inward from the high central profile. If the flat center of the stone was used to place the profile line, plenty of volume and labor would be lost in creating a profile in the center when it already exists at the corner.

As soon as the flat top of the stone was changed to a domelike shape by using the pitch tool and the point, I had no further use for the pitching tool. Points and chisels are the tools that will shape the stone. With a medium point ⅜-inch in diameter and 7½ inches long, I have begun to break through the corners to the left and right of the central high line. The charcoal markings in Figure 3–11 indicate the secondary high points along the cheeks. Notice that these are further inward than the center line. Although the slopes on either side of the stone are suggesting shoulders, it would be a mistake at this early stage to make any decisions on shoulders

FIGURE 3–11   The horizontal line indicates the position of the eyes. The vertical line at the center is the highest point of the sculpture. (Photo by Gil McMillon)

before the head is clear. In order to clear the head from the block, it will be necessary to carve right through what seems to be shoulders in Figure 3–11. The horizontal mark indicates where the eyes may be located later. Much of the top corners of the stone has been carved through and away in the attempt and need to get the circular movement of the head out of the cube shape of the stone. The first central high point charcoal mark remains; it had to be constantly redrawn during the carving. During carving, it is necessary to carve upon the chalk marks but to redraw them in order to help yourself stay on course. The decision to place the next high points at the cheeks is influenced by the observation that, after the nose, moving horizontally, the next steep turn in the head is at the cheeks and at points on the forehead. Notice that outlines against space have appeared where the high point lines along the cheeks are drawn. When carving, it is important to carve inward at the points where the planes change direction. When observing objects, changes in the direction of the planes can be detected by the outlines against space and also by the boundaries between light and shade. The shape of an outline between light and shade describes the route along which the planes turn. The same is true of outlines against space. With this in mind, the direct carver creates forms by controlling their exterior outlines against space and their interior reflection of light and shade.

Although I have drawn a horizontal line indicating the position of the eyes, I have not attempted to carve them. A common error among beginners is to "carve out" the eyes by scooping out a hollow where the eyes are to be. But eyes are full positive forms. Observe closed eyes, and you will see the true forms. But even if there are to be hollows, it is best to keep the form bulging before creating the hollows. In Figure 3–11, I have not defined the hollows that exist between the nose and the mouth, the mouth and the chin, or the chin and the neck. These hollows will remain undefined to enable me to carve from the highest to the lowest forms without widening the hollows. When the hollows are carved out too soon, they deepen and widen as the sculpture develops; and when this happens, parts that should touch move apart. The nose, mouth, chin, and neck must relate to each other, with proper spaces between them. And to ensure this, all negative spaces are being treated as positive—not hollow—forms. I have begun to use three- and five-tooth claw chisels, as well as the point. The chisels are being used to give me a closer feel of the stone. With the chisel pressed firmly against the stone, I can glide over the forms and shape them, particularly the bulge of the forehead and the egglike forms of the first stages of the eyes. There is no danger of removing too much stone in this early stage; but if enough is not removed, the work will be flat.

The photograph of the work in progress, Figure 3–12, shows a profile. The arrow points to the untouched exterior corner of the stone where the central high point was placed. A deep indentation has been made to establish the relationship between

FIGURE 3–12 The profile shows the depth of the undercuts. The arrow points to the original exterior corner of the stone where the central highest points of the sculpture are located. (Photo by Gil McMillon)

the tip of nose and the base of neck, from the highest point to the lowest. Relating these two points is important in order to find and place the forms in between them, such as the mouth and the chin. The arrow also points to a mass of stone that I plan to use as a hand.

Figure 3–13 shows the same profile as in Figure 3–12. The eye is being rounded as it should be. When looking at an eye in profile, the reason one corner is out of the line of vision is that the eye turns sharply inward from the center. In Figure 3–13 the first tentative separation is made between the tip of the nose and the stone mass; a negative space has been made. The cheek is beginning to appear without the need of a chalkline to define it. This was done by carving inward from the high point line of the cheek toward the nose. The vertical charcoal line running down the center of the stone clearly shows that the sculpture has moved in an arc through three corners of the stone in order to describe half a circle, a necessary motion in extricating three-dimensional sculpture from cubelike stones.

FIGURE 3–13 The profile develops. The eye is being rounded as it should be, and the first tentative separation of the nose from the rest of the stone mass is made. (Photo by Gil McMillon)

Now that the main blocking-out of the sculpture has been done and firm decisions have been made as to the locations of features, it is time to be specific about the modeling. The features to be carved are chalked in black lines (see Figure 3–14). Although I have outlined the mouth, no separation is made between the upper and lower lips. All touching forms must be carved primarily as a single form in order to allow rounding. If touching forms are separated while flat, rounding will be impossible, since chiseling will cause the separation between the forms to widen, and what is to be a closed mouth in this case will open and cease to relate to the other features. Superficial observation concludes that the mouth is a parallel line from corner to corner. However, the shape of the mouth is a curve from one corner to the next. When a face is seen in profile, the other corner of the mouth cannot be seen because it is around a bend. I have not concerned myself with any definitions of a hairline, ears, or a base. Such definitions are to be avoided in the early stages of a sculpture. They are inhibiting to the progress of the piece, for there is a tendency to stop carving at such landmarks (see Figure 3–15).

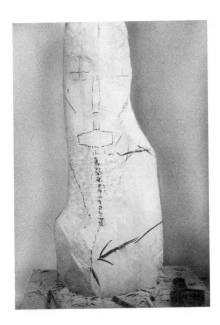

FIGURE 3–14 The features to be carved are chalked in black outlines. The arrow points to the corner used as the central high point of the sculpture. (Photo by Gil McMillon)

FIGURE 3–15 The sculpture is almost completed. The chalkiness on the right show the hand, which was shifted from its original position in the center of the stone. (Photo by Gil McMillon)

I once had a student who proposed to carve a head for his first venture into direct carving. He drew a heavy chalkline 6 inches from the top of the stone and called it the hairline. Next, he drew a line to the left and one to the right, marking the ear-lines. Finally, he located the baseline 6 inches above the bottom of the stone, and no one could persuade him to make any excursions around or through those lineal fixations. The results were predictable. As he carved, strictly observing the boundary lines, the head sank deeper into the stone, becoming smaller; whereas the hair, ears, and base, protected by their boundaries, became ponderous attachments. One felt sorry for the head under such pressure.

The art of carving is most successful when the details are added to the masses instead of the reverse. Some sculptors draw four sides of a proposed sculpture upon four sides of the stone to be carved. The drawings are intended to indicate the positions of the front, back, left, and right sides of the piece. Avoid this natural bad habit, because as soon as the carving away of stone begins, the subtraction inward bypasses all that surface drawing. The sculptor with drawings on four sides of the stone, then, spends the remaining carving time subtracting inward with chisels while trying to preserve the drawings on the exterior—a frustrating improbability that is quite visible on the finished sculptures. Try to keep your work flowing past all the sides so that all views offer a design that is exciting to look at (see Figure 3–16).

Carvers place chalk marks upon the surface of the material being carved during the entire carving process. These chalk marks are used as guidelines from which the sculptor carves inward. The outlines of a drawing on a flat surface define the limits of the visual presentation of that particular drawing. But the same outlines on a carving merely indicate the end of one plane and the beginning of the next; unlike the two-dimensional drawing, the next plane is continued. The observer of a three-dimensional carving can walk around the sculpture and see past the outlines. The sculptor considers outlines to be pauses between the angling planes. A piece of sculpture directly carved in the round describes an

FIGURE 3–16 A profile of the head in limestone, finished in the rough— that is, the chisel and point marks are left unsanded. No attempt has been made to smooth any parts. (Photo by Gil McMillon)

infinite number of views and has no lineal boundaries.

The sculpture of a head in limestone is now complete. One shoulder had to be sacrificed in order to support the head with a neck sufficient in length and grace (see Figure 3–17). An important frame of mind for the carver is flexibility. When we think of a sculpture of a head, it is natural to expect it to have a neck and then shoulders. In sculpture that allows additions, all things are possible, including the unnecessary, but extricating a sculpture by subtracting from a solid mass very often forces the carver to relinquish nonessentials. Notice that the hand that was earlier intended to appear in the center has been omitted in order to increase the length of the neck (see Figure 3–18 for the sequence of construction).

The sculpture is finished without polish, and tool marks add texture. This piece will be refined in Chapter 5, when polishing and finishing will be demonstrated.

FIGURE 3–17 The sculpture of the head is now complete. One shoulder had to be sacrificed in order to support the head with a neck sufficient in length and grace. (Photo by Gil McMillon)

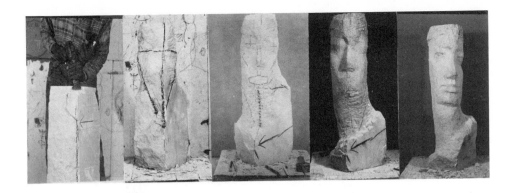

FIGURE 3-18 A sequence of stages, showing the transformation from block of stone to sculpture. (Photos by Gil McMillon)

The remarkable sculpture of a salamander in Figure 13-19, by Paul Daigneault, is a very successful stone carving. This sculpture is made remarkable because it was the artist's first attempt at stonecarving. The forms are wrapped around and also thrust through the block of stone. This twisting of the forms to conform within the confines of the block is evident when one observes that the spine or high point of the sculpture starts at the back of the head of the salamander and twists through and around the block, reappearing at the front, where it began. When it reappears at the front, it appears in the form of the tail. This "snaking" of the high point in order to fit the length of the salamander into the confines of the block of limestone is one of the fine points of carving an unlimited form from a limited

other examples of stonecarving

FIGURE 3–19 *Salamander* by Paul Daigneault.
(Photo by Gil McMillon)

block of material. The smooth, globelike shape
seen at right in Figure 3–19, is an egg, which was
discovered as the sculptor cleared his way into the
block in search of shapes. The finish left chisel
marks to contrast with the smooth egg and eyes of
the sculpture of a salamander.

The limestone block from which Tayo Heuser
carved *Snarling Cat* measured 24 inches high and
19 inches wide but was only 8 inches thick (see
Figure 3–20). Notice that Tayo Heuser carved
straight through the block of stone and, in so
doing, increased its narrow 8-inch thickness and
produced the huge, voluminous head of the snarling cat, which seems larger in volume than the
block from which it came. This ability to increase
the volume of stone available for carving by opening up its interior is crucial to successful carving.
The opposite to opening up the stone is to skirt
around the exterior, creating a flat sculpture that
maintains the original shape of the stone. Skirting
around the exterior is the wrong way. The block
has all of the sculpture contained; to reveal the

FIGURE 3–20 *Snarling Cat* by Tayo Heuser. The ability to increase the volume of the stone available for carving by opening up its interior is crucial to successful carving. (Photo by Gil McMillon)

FIGURE 3–21 *Snarling Cat.* The side view shows the great extent of the deep undercutting. (Photo by Gil McMillon)

sculpture contained in the block, one must open it up.

Figure 3–21 (side view) of *Snarling Cat* shows the great extent of deep undercutting executed by the sculptor in order to reveal the contents of the stone. In this case, the undercut began at the tip of the nose of the cat and moved in and down to the base of the neck, a distance of 1½ feet. This undercut revealed or discovered the mouth, teeth, chin, neck, and, finally, the claws of the *Snarling Cat*; all of these features were exposed as the sculptor cleaved into and through the stone. There is always a risk of the stone breaking during the execution of strong undercuts. However, this risk is less so in limestone than in marble or alabaster. Sharp tools minimize the risk of fracturing the stone.

Stone is not as easily pinned and joined as wood. Many sculptors attempt to carve stone in sections and then join the sections to make a whole, often with good results.

The torso in Figure 3–22 by Charles Grossman would not have its particular charm if it had been carved from a single block. The piece is comprised of three sections, and the joints are deliberately unconcealed. A masonry bit was used to drill ⅜-inch holes into the limestone sections. In the upper and lower sections, the holes are 3 inches deep. In the

FIGURE 3–22 *Torso* by Charles Grossman. (Photo by Chee Heng Yeong)

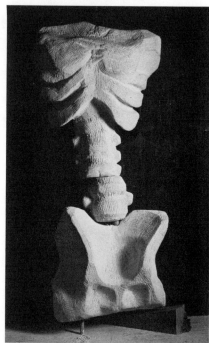

middle section, the hole went clear through. Steel rods ⅜-inch in diameter and epoxy glue hold all together.

These examples of stonecarving should give you an idea of some of the possibilities inherent in stone.

4

**carving
marble and
alabaster**

marble THE brittle, crystallized nature of marble causes it to be easily bruised during the carving process. Bruising the marble is one of the common errors made by the beginner. It is a natural error; the marble is hard, and force, it is thought, must be used. The truth is that the more force you use, the more resistance you meet. Bruises or crushed crystals on the marble surface appear as streaks, frosted dots, or lines, and these show clearly when the stone is polished. Such bruises mar the finished sculpture. On white marble, bruises would appear to be whiter than the white of the stone. On gray marble, scars would appear as lighter gray or whitish gray. On all marbles, the crushed crystals can be easily recognized, for they appear as discordant pock marks. Removing crushed crystals is laborious, especially since some crush marks are well below the surface, reaching depths of half an inch or more, depending upon the force of the blow that caused them.

The harder properties of marble require greater use of the point to shape the sculpture. The claw chisels are not very effective on marble except when gliding over inroads made by the point. Some of the important considerations to observe in order to avoid bruising the surface of marble are the size of the points used, the angle at which the point is held against the marble, and the force of the hammer blows. Slender points are best for use on marble. Stout points meet much resistance, which in turn encourages heavy hammering. The combination of too much force and a stout point will bruise the marble.

The angle at which the point is held against the stone should never be 90°—that is, the point should never be driven straight into the marble. Instead, it should be glanced off the marble, making shallow grooves. After many shallow grooves are cross-hatched, the shape of the marble will begin to change and yield to your intentions.

The hammer should not be swung as if driving a nail. Hold the hammer halfway down on the handle toward the hammerhead and tap lightly. This is all the force needed to drive the slender, sharp point through the surface of the marble. The marble changes shape under the carver's tools, not so much by fracturing off chunks but by interlacing the stone with point grooves.

If, in spite of precautions, some bruises occur, these can be removed before the sculpture is polished. The method of removing crushed crystal markings in the finishing stages is described in Chapter 5.

Marble should not be attempted for a first carving. Experience should be gained carving the softer limestone before attempting to carve marble. Eye and face protectors must be worn at all times when carving marble; the splintered fragments are sharp. Use a face mask as well as goggles. Goggles alone do not protect the cheeks.

the carving process
working with marble

Start with a piece of marble small enough so that two persons can lift it onto a work table yet heavy enough to withstand carving without sliding or bouncing. If the stone weighs only 20 to 50 pounds, it will fall over or move with the impact of the tools. Although clamping and other expediencies can be used to hold a light piece of stone in place, it is best to avoid extra problems in a first piece. Start with a marble from 100 pounds up to 200 pounds in weight. Marble weighs about 180 pounds per cubic foot. Start the first marble sculpture with a piece that measures at least a cubic foot, an ideal weight and volume to enable a beginner to concentrate on the new experiences of discovery.

If the stone is a small piece and needs bracing, there are a few ways to do it. The quickest way is to place the stone in a bench vise attached to the work table. Turn the stone and reclamp it as often as necessary. This is not, however, the best technique, for it is hard to see the whole work at once.

Sandbags are another device for stabilizing small stones. Make a sandbag by stitching together three sides of two squares of any thick cloth, fill the bag three-quarters full with sand, and then stitch the fourth side. Place the sandbag on the work table to serve as a cradle for the small marble. The sandbag not only stabilizes the stone but also muffles the sounds of the tools, a good system if one has a studio where others may be disturbed by noise from a thumping hammer.

The use of molding plaster is the best method of stabilizing smaller marbles for carving. Molding plaster is sometimes called plaster of Paris. I hesitate to label it by that name because a spackling compound for house painters, sold at hardware stores, is called plaster of Paris, and it will not serve the sculptor's needs in this case. Molding plaster is obtainable at sculpture or potters' suppliers or at art supply stores. Sometimes these suppliers will order the plaster on request if they do not stock it. The plaster powder must be mixed with water before it is usable. The mix of plaster and water must be equal parts by volume. Many substances are of entirely different weights even though their volumes are equal, and the weights of water and plaster at equal volumes are about 16 ounces of water to 48 ounces of plaster. However, artists have found a way to bypass the tedium of weighing as a way to ensure the proper mix of plaster to water. Here is how. If your mixing container is a 12-ounce coffee can, half fill it with water. Sprinkle plaster into the water, small quantities at a time, with no pauses during the sprinkling of the plaster. Keep sprinkling the plaster into the water until it rises to the surface and begins to make islands of plaster at water level. Continue to add more plaster between the islands until the plaster displaces the water and all is an ooze of plaster saturated by water. It is important never to stir the mix while adding the plaster to the water. Any stirring will disturb the mix, the plaster build-up will sink, and the system of mixing equal parts by volume without weighing will be inaccurate if it is stirred before all the plaster is sprinkled in and has risen to the surface. Never add water to plaster. Always add the plaster powder to water when mixing.

When water and plaster are equal, using the mixing system described above, stir the mixture with a stick or paddle. Do not attempt to crush the lumps. The lumps will do no harm, and time spent crushing them will be time lost, for you have less than 25 minutes to use the mix before it sets solid.

Burlap cut into small pieces is needed to add strength to the plaster. Because of the rapidity with which the plaster sets, it is advisable to cut the burlap into small pieces, about 3" x 5", before mixing the plaster. As soon as the plaster is mixed, dip a piece of burlap in plaster and then press the burlap against the base of the stone, trailing a part of the burlap onto the table. This action serves to tie the stone to the table. Repeat the process, working rapidly around the base of the marble and moving no more than about 2 inches upward. When the plaster becomes too thick to saturate the burlap, apply the thick plaster with a spackle knife, packing it outward from the base of the marble. Make a new mix if necessary and repeat the process until you are satisfied that the marble has a good footing. At least four hours must pass after applying plaster to the base of the marble before carving can proceed. When the sculpture has progressed to completion, chip off the plaster.

The Vermont marble carved for this demonstration was found on one of my searches at a building demolition site. The stone is white with light green veins. It could have been a fireplace embellishment, for it has not been exposed to the weather. It measures 16 inches high, 8 inches wide, and 5 inches deep.

The tools I have chosen are not very different from the tools used to carve limestone, except that I have chosen to use only very slender points ¼ inch in diameter and about 7½ inches long. I have three of these for this project, one three-tooth claw chisel, and a broad chisel with five teeth.

The reason for using three points is that the hardness of marble blunts the tips of the points sooner than softer stones, and frequent sharpening is necessary (see Chapter 1 on how to sharpen stone tools). Claw chisels require less sharpening than points because their uses are for grading or refining rather than for breaking into the stone, as the points must.

I have deliberately omitted any flat or finishing chisels at the start of the work. The early inclusion of finishing chisels encourages their premature use, which in turn causes the user to arrive before getting there. The reason that too-early use of finishing tools acts against proper development of the sculpture is that finishing chisels are incapable of breaking into stone. They are designed for shallow grading. When flat finishing chisels are used at the very early stages of the work, the surface of the stone becomes prematurely smoothed, giving the impression that the work is finished.

The sculpture of a head in gray marble shown in Figure 4–1 demonstrates an example of obtaining the forms with a minimum of removal of material. The top of the sculpture remains unchanged, almost as the block of marble was before carving. Most of the modeling was done with a minimum of subtraction of materials. Parts of the stone surface are smoothed, whereas other areas are left with

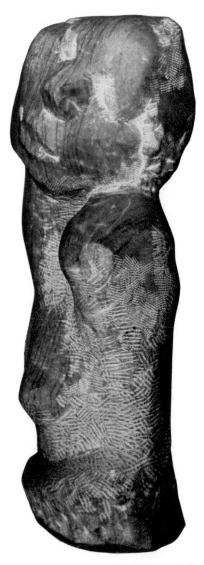

FIGURE 4–1 Head in
gray Vermont marble by
Arnold Prince. (Private
collection. Chris Bebee,
New Zealand; photo
supplied by the author)

chisel marks. This combination of texture and
smooth surface is very desirable.

Either a totally smooth or a totally textured surface
is equally acceptable, depending upon the piece
and the sculptor. The important thing is not to finish
the surface too early. Premature finish surfaces are
especially undesirable for beginners, who are usually inhibited from breaking into the material in
search of new forms and different possibilities.

sculpting the preening cat

Just before carving this marble, I'd bought two drawings of cats from an artist friend. There were two pages, with eight drawings of cats on each page. The interesting point of these drawings was that the cats were not posing, as in so many cat drawings, but were busy doing what cats do when they are not sleeping—eating and preening. I chose one of the preening poses for this sculpture, and with that decision, I began to stalk the family cat in order to improve my observations. The charm of my friend's drawings of cats preening was that he had captured the act with a great deal of candor.

The drawing shows one side of the cat preening, but the sculpture must explore all of the other views. Instead of creating drawings of all of the possibilities of the work in the round, I prefer to have a drawing of one view only and to leave all other aspects of the form to discovery (see Figure 4–2). It is hampering to the carver to have it all worked out either in a drawing or in a clay model and then set out to copy it. The stone will not comply, and when forced, the result appears contrived.

Figures 4–2 and 4–3 show that the sculpture has begun to disagree with the drawing by showing many different planes or levels. In the drawing, the tail is extended outward, but in the sculpture, the tail is wrapped around to conform to the shape of the stone. This adaptation of the plan to fit the material is not a handicap. Instead, it has a cleansing effect upon the design; the limitations force the sculptor to drop the trimmings. The point was used to break into the block and change it from a cube, causing it to take on the profile of the drawing (see Figures 4–4 and 4–5 for further views of the sculpture).

alabaster

Carving alabaster always reminds me of the name given to pottery in one of the Caribbean Islands on which I grew up. In Antigua, West Indies, the pot-

FIGURE 4–2 The drawing shows one side of the cat preening, but the sculpture must explore all of the other views. (Photo by Gordon Cruz)

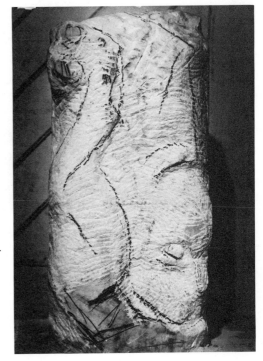

FIGURE 4–3 The sculpture of the cat preening is now becoming more defined. The charcoal lines at the extreme left outline the raised leg. Note the busy chisel texture that indents the marble surface. Compare this with Figure 4–2 and observe how the sculpture has progressed from the flat surface of the marble toward the interior. (Photo by Gordon Cruz)

tery pieces used for charcoal cooking are known as coalpots, or *omigod*. I did not understand the slang as a child until one day my mother sent me to the market to buy an *omigod* to be used for the family cooking that day. On my way home with the earthenware, I accidentally stepped on a strewn mango skin, slipped, and fell. The ceramic coalpot I carried broke in pieces with that special spite with which ceramics break. Devastated, I cried, "O my God!" Sometimes during the cooking the coalpots may open up and spill the dinner, causing the same exclamation.

The reclining figure in Colorado alabaster by Tayo

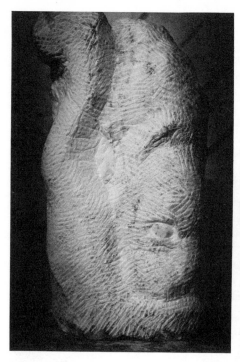

FIGURE 4–4   The same view as in Figure 4–3, only here the charcoal markings of the raised leg have been carved in depth by carving into the interior of the marble, using the charcoal lines as a guide from which to carve inward. A three-tooth chisel is the major tool for modeling. (Photo by Gordon Cruz)

FIGURE 4–5   The marble sculpture of the cat preening finished in the rough, with working chisel marks providing a lively texture. Notice that the drawing, which showed one side only, has been expanded by the sculpture in the round. Compare this with Figure 4–2. (Photo by Gordon Cruz)

Heuser shown in Figure 4–6 demonstrates that large volumes can be obtained from small scale works. The piece is slightly over 15 inches in length and about 8 inches at its highest point. By using relative scale and by carving completely in the round, the sculptor bypassed the limited confines of the stone. One sees clear through and into space at the points of contact between the sculpture and the ground or base. The sculpture has been polished, and all tool marks have been eliminated. The dark markings are veins, which contribute much to the beauty of alabaster; however, the sculptor must avoid carving straight into these veins, since the stone can break at veins or flaws.

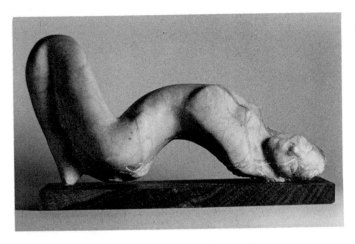

FIGURE 4–6 *Reclining Figure* by Tayo Heuser (Private collection, Bernard Mendor, Rhode Island; photo by Chee Heng Yeong)

Observe an alabaster boulder carefully before carving it. There is no reason to eliminate a boulder if it has a visible crack. It depends on where the crack is. If it is near an edge or corner, it would be simple to break it off before starting the sculpture. A good practice is to mark any flaws with a charcoal; then, during the carving, make sure to carve across the flaws without embedding the tool in the flaw. With the right handling, most of the veins will hold as they are. I have carved dozens of alabaster boulders without encountering any extra problems once care and awareness are applied. Too often, inexperienced carvers will probe into a vein "to see what happens." Well, what will happen is that the vein will separate if it gets special attention from the tools.

The tools required to carve alabaster are points and claw chisels, plus flat chisels for finishing. The pitching tool is unnecessary for this softest of stones. Bruising happens easily, and much care should be exercised by using as little force as possible. The claw chisels are very important in carving alabaster. Because of its softness, pointing is used minimally, and much of the work can be chiseled.

the carving process
working with alabaster

Alabaster can be carved with a great deal of detail. Avoid clear-through holes as part of the design. The stone is weak and will break from stress when holes are bored or carved through it. Undercuts can be deep and should stop short of going through.

sculpting the goose in flight

The Colorado alabaster boulder shown in Figure 4-7 rested in my studio for more than a year. It is 20 inches high, 25 inches broad, and measures 13 inches thick at the base, tapering to only 4 inches thick at the top. It weighs about 200 pounds.

I have a specific subject in mind for this sculpture in alabaster, but I shall leave the details to chance. I shall plan only the main theme of the subject and seize opportunities offered during the carving to make specific decisions. In this way, the design will be in sympathy with the nature of the stone. My

FIGURE 4-7 The Colorado alabaster boulder rested in my studio for more than a year. It is 20 inches high, 25 inches broad, and measures 13 inches thick at the base, tapering to only 4 inches at the top. It weighs about 200 pounds. The charcoal line at the top will be used as a point from which to carve inward to create the graceful arch of the back of a bird in flight. (Photo by Gordon Cruz)

plan is to carve an aquatic bird in flight, preferably a goose. The idea came as I looked at the arch of the top of the boulder. I have drawn a charcoal line at the top of the back and the outthrust neck of a bird in flight.

In Figure 4–8, I have started to carve inward from the main high point. The three sweeping lines at the center of the stone suggest the sweep of a wing. The round dot indicates the eye and serves to help me obtain a feel for the head at the end of a neck, thrust out in flight. The next step will be to move from flat lines to incised and carved forms. This view of the block will be called side #1; the opposite side will be called side #2.

With point and chisel, the sculpture of a goose in flight has begun to take shape (see Figure 4–9). From the initial lines indicating head and neck, the forward thrusting head and neck are becoming clearer. These forms are obtained by carving straight into the stone. There is a constant temptation to carve straight through to the other side in

FIGURE 4–8 The three sweeping lines at the center of the stone suggest the sweep of a wing. The round dot at the right indicates the eye. (Photo by Gordon Cruz)

FIGURE 4–9 With point and chisel, the
sculpture of a goose in flight has begun to take
shape. (Photo by Gordon Cruz)

order to free the neck and head from the rest of the
stone, but this would be a mistake. Were a clear-
through negative space carved at the lower line of
the neck, the top of the stone would collapse. Ties,
such as those in a stencil, must be maintained
when undercutting in alabaster. I plan to carve
deeply along the charcoal line indicating the base
of the head and the neck, but I shall stop short of
breaking completely through.

Not only is the head more clearly defined at this
stage, but a wing design is developing (see Figure
4–10). Notice the extensive use of the claw chisels.
Because of the softness of the alabaster, the points
are not used as often as the claw chisels. Whenever new and drastic cuttings must be done, the
point is the tool to use. But in this soft stone, a five-
tooth claw chisel can do half of the blocking out of
the form. The point marks beneath the head of the
flying goose indicate a need to penetrate the stone
deeply in that spot, which required the point. The
sculptor should shift tools as demanded by the sit-
uation.

FIGURE 4-10 Not only is the head more clearly defined at this stage but a wing design is developing. (Photo by Gordon Cruz)

I plan to carve under the neck deeply enough to create a strong negative undercut, which in turn will accent the positive form of the neck. But the undercut must stop short of going through to the other side. Such a clear-through cut would cause the neck to collapse from the top, bringing on one of those alabaster calamities. It would be safe to free the beak and head from the rest of the stone, but only after making sure that all the heavy hammering at the top is finished.

So far, we have been looking at one side of the stone. The sculpture is to be in the round. Having made sure that the substance of the subject chosen is quite feasible, I have started to move the form around, past the head of the flying goose, and to define it so clearly by carving that it no longer depends on the charcoal drawing. This can be seen in Figure 4-11: Here, the head of the goose has assumed many dimensions.

Using the center chalk line as the middle of the form from which all the other forms move back or

FIGURE 4–11 The head of the goose has assumed many dimensions; it is no longer flat. (Photo by Gordon Cruz)

FIGURE 4–12 Moving around one end of the stone past the head of the goose, I now confront size #2 of the stone and will change it from a side into an integral part of a sculpture in the round. (Photo by Gordon Cruz)

FIGURE 4–13 The sculpture of the goose in flight is now at a stage of rough finish. (Photo by Gordon Cruz)

inward, I have begun to cut into the block in order to discover the shapes not yet revealed. At the same time, and still using the central line as a pivot, I have started to move past the head and into side #2 of the stone. There is a great temptation to carve away the stone under the beak of the goose so that the head can float free and give the feeling of flight, but this must wait. If the underside of the stone is removed too early, then hammering at the top will cause the projected portion of the stone to break off. Hold the deep undercuts and wait until the upper parts are nearly finished before undermining. Moving around one end of the stone past the head of the goose, I now confront side #2 of the stone and will change it from a side into an integral part of a sculpture in the round. The charcoal lines are guides from which to cut (see Figure 4–12). The sculpture will be symmetrical, as it is to be a sculpture of a bird in flight, yet the sides will not be exact duplicates of each other (see Figure 4–13 for a view of the rough-finished sculpture).

5

**polishing
and finishing
stone**

ALL stones are polishable. It has always surprised students of stone carving that limestone, which shows no signs of shiny crystals, can be polished to a high sheen equal to that of marble. Although we are dealing here with three main types of stone—marble, alabaster, and limestone—the systems described, including polishing, are applicable to all stones. A sculpture in stone can be finished by removing some or all texture, according to the design. The work can also be left in the rough, exactly as the tools left it. Unpolished stone carvings have a peculiar beauty. But, like so many things, there are other sides to the matter, and some sculptures are improved, even enhanced, by polish. Polishing enriches the colors of the stone and seals the surface, enabling it to resist soil. Sculptures in stone can be completely or partially polished. The latter is a very interesting use of polish, since the partially polished portions show off the polished portions by contrast. There are no rules on whether or not the sculpture should be polished. It is entirely up to the artist. Give the decision much thought, because polishing requires removing most or all of the textures, and once the working textures or tool marks have been removed, they can never be replaced in order to show how they occurred during the rush to shape the sculpture (see Figures 5–1, 5–2, and 5–3 for examples of polished pieces).

A sure way of discovering what the sculpture will look like when polished is to wet it thoroughly by pouring water over it until no dry spots are left. The wet stone closely forecasts the color and sheen that the polished stone will have. Anyone who has visited the seashore will notice that the pebbles wet by the sea are deeper in color than the dry pebbles out of the sea's reach. Those dry pebbles can be polished to maintain the colors of the wet ones.

how to polish stone The tools for polishing stone are remarkably simple (see Figure 5–4). First, you will need a piece of carborundum stone, which is available at hardware

FIGURE 5–1 *Pelican* by Catherine Lebel Schaefer. A fine example of polishing Vermont marble to enhance the carved forms. (Photo by Gil McMillon)

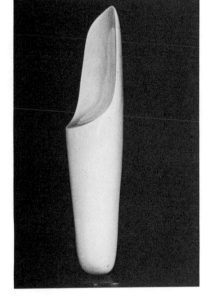

FIGURE 5–2 *Shell Form #1* by Shelly Robzen. This very highly polished sculpture of carrara marble is a good example of the need to polish certain kinds of forms completely. (Photo by the artist)

FIGURE 5–3 *Weltschmerz* by Ann Jon. A stunning piece of Bardiglio marble enhanced by the combination of smooth and textured surfaces. (Private collection; photo by Studio Fotografico, I Bessi, Carrara, Italy)

FIGURE 5–4 Some of the simple tools used to
polish and finish stone sculpture. From left to right,
1¼-inch flat chisel, ¾-inch flat chisel, ⅝-inch flat
chisel, ⅜-inch flat chisel, riffler file for filing details.
(Photo by Gordon Cruz)

stores in coarse, medium, and fine grades. Only
marble requires all grades. For limestone and alabaster, use medium and fine grades only. Next, a
metal file, preferably one that has both coarse and
fine filing textures. A sculptor's riffler, available at
art supply stores, is used for details.

Crushed crystals or bruises which occur as a result
of the carving process must be removed before the
stone sculpture can be properly polished. If the
sculpture is polished without removing the bruises,
the surface of the work will be marred. Removing
crushed crystals is not a matter of choice but a
must.

To identify crushed crystals, remove all texture from
the areas where polish is desired, using a flat

chisel, and pour water over the work. When the stone is wet, the crushed crystals will appear as chalky white pock marks regardless of the color of the stone.

To remove the bruises continue to carve over them with a sharp chisel. In some cases the crystals may be crushed to a depth of half an inch; in which case half an inch of stone must be removed before the material is blemish-free. Filing the stone with a metal rasp is a slower way of removing bruises. Too much filing can change some subtle forms. The sculptor is more in control and can maintain the shape of the work when removing crushed crystals with a flat chisel.

Polishing is essentially a filing and sanding operation. The best sandpaper for polishing is carbide sandpaper, known in hardware stores as "wet and dry" sandpaper; and for this purpose the sandpaper should always be used wet. Obtain the wet and dry sandpaper in grades 220A (coarse), 320A (medium), and 400A–600A (fine).

Recently, an abrasive sanding screen has appeared on the market at sculpture and art supply stores. The grades of the screen are similar to those of the wet and dry paper. Use of the screen with or instead of the sandpaper is optional. If the screen is used instead of the sandpaper, be sure to use the 600A fine sandpaper as a final sander. A flat chisel, ½-inch to 1-inch in width, is the only chisel needed for the finishing process. It removes the texture and prepares the way for the files and sandpaper.

Finally, a polishing agent is applied. Polishing agents are acids or powdered compounds that, when applied and rubbed into the smoothed surface of the stone, cause it to seal and glisten. Of all the polishing agents, my preference is a powder called tin oxide, which is available at ceramic or sculpture suppliers. If the sculpture was carved from a block of stone measuring one cubic foot, then two ounces of tin oxide will be enough for the polish. Start the polishing by smoothing the surface of the sculpture, removing only undesired texture. The flat chisel is the best tool for removing bruises that may mar the polish. Some sculptors start the smoothing with files, but a flat chisel will accomplish in a single pass what many minutes of filing is required in order to do. On alabaster, the files tend to leave hard-to-remove scratches, so it is advisable to use files only on hard stones.

After the surface is smoothed by the flat chisel, proceed to file with a medium to fine file, assisted by the carborundum stone. Occasionally, wet the work in order to see your progress. When wet, scars and rough spots will be clearly visible. Mark these with charcoal. Then proceed when the stone dries. Water on the stone will dry off rapidly. Use the carborundum stone in a filing motion. The stone can be wet when using the abrasive stone.

When the sculpture is smooth to the touch, it is time for the wet and dry sandpaper. For alabaster or other soft stone, start with 400A and finish with 600A. Marble or limestone requires from 200A coarse through the finest grade available. The sanding prior to the polish is time-consuming. Wear a rubber glove. I have seen students of sculpture sand away the skin on their fingertips.

Prolonged use of the carbide sandpapers brings out the beauty of the stone. Limestone, which is very light colored in its unpolished state, will begin to assume a deep tone as the length of the sanding increases. In marble and alabaster, hues and colors that were invisible will now be seen. Postpone the final tin oxide application until the work is absolutely smooth. Portions where texture is desired should be rubbed with the carborundum in order to flatten any sharp ridges without losing the texture. Sand over the textured portions with coarse and fine carbide paper. During all of the sanding, the work should be kept wet, or at least the spot being sanded should be wet. I keep a container of warm water on the work table in which I dip the sandpaper.

Take care not to soften any sharp features of the work during the polishing. The aim should be to heighten these. It may be necessary to rechisel parts of the sculpture. Very often, the polish shows up weaknesses that can be redefined. The sanding operation does not have to begin and end in a day. The longer the process, the better the polish. Extend the sanding as long as there is time. I polish a piece as I am working on and around many other projects, for it is tedious work.

The stone gives a clear signal that it is time to apply the polishing agent. You can see this signal when the surface remains deep-toned as if wet, even though the material is dry, and when it begins to sheen when rubbed with the palm. These conditions will start after much use of the 600A carbide paper, and when they appear, it is time to apply tin oxide. Pour an ounce of tin oxide powder in a waterproof container (it is a poison, so do not use an eating or drinking vessel). Mix enough water with the powder to produce a light paste similar to the consistency of liquid shoe polish. With a piece of felt or a polishing cloth, rub the tin oxide paste vigorously over the wet surface. Rub in a concentrated way—one area at a time—and keep as much pressure as possible on the rubbing pad. Once the tin oxide is applied to the surface, do not rinse it off when wetting is required. Instead, wet the polishing pad. For as long as the tin oxide is needed, its presence on the stone surface can be extended by redampening the pad. If the sculpture was well sanded, the action of the tin oxide will complete the polish. Using the 200-pound block, as we have, for a guide, the tin oxide should be rubbed for about an hour. Rinse off all the tin oxide with a liberal pouring of water or, if it is small enough, place the sculpture in a sink. Let dry. The piece can now be buffed to produce the sheen. Buffing is done with a piece of felt or by placing a buffing pad on a high-speed drill. Buffing pads for hand use or for drills are sold at hardware stores. The buffing pad on a drill will not alter the forms of the sculpture and is a way of producing the amount of friction needed for a high polish without expending too much physical energy. Chamois is a good buffing cloth if felt is not available.

6

**carving
wood**

types of wood best suited for carving

ALL wood can be carved. Such a broad statement, though true, does not help the sculptor to select the best woods for carving. An attempt is made here to present a guide to the more carvable woods, for some woods are more satisfying to carve than others. Availability often determines which kind of wood the sculptor carves, which is the best determining factor of all. Sculptors who have worked only in stone will not only find woodcarving closely related to it but will also be well prepared to carve wood after the stonecarving experience. Some of the rewards of carving wood, after carving only stone, are the greater range of options offered by wood and its lesser weight.

The comparatively lighter weight of wood enables the woodcarver to work on a massive scale without having to deal with the enormous weights that would be involved in stone of similar measurements. Wood carvings also lend themselves well to additions by gluing and pinning. Wood can also be laminated, that is, joined with tough glues, and mixed for color complements and contrasts. Woodcarving is alive, free, and open.

All of this does not mean that wood is a better medium than stone. Both materials enrich the sculptor's choices. A sculptor who works in both media, wood and stone, will find that the experience serves to improve carving skills and that it also broadens the range of professional expertise. Holes and openings or negative spaces moving clear through are feasible in wood sculpture without the risk of fracturing that is always present in stone. Because of its fibrous nature, wood is a strong material.

Hardwoods can be identified as the wood of trees that lose their leaves in winter, and softwoods are the evergreens. This is a very general description of the woods found in temperate climates, and there are exceptions. Another paradox of the term for the sculptor is that hardwood or softwood does not mean harder or softer. I have carved hardwoods that are easy to carve, and I have encountered some tough softwoods. Woods available for carving vary according to country; in some countries, they vary with the regions. In the United States, the native hardwood logs most commonly available are oaks and maples. Birch, beech, walnut, butternut, chestnut, and applewood—or any fruit-tree wood—are also available. Elm, ash, hickory, eucalyptus, and locust are also carvable hardwoods of great beauty. Cherry is a popular hardwood with carvers because of its ruby-reddish color. The list can go on, but the above includes the most available woods.

Softwoods suitable for carving are spruce, pine, fir, and red or white cedars. Redwood is an excellent softwood for carving, but it is hardly ever attainable in log form. However, it can be carved by laminating boards. Basswood and willow are very soft woods, although they cannot classify as softwoods from a botanist's point of view. But for the sculptor's information, both woods offer little resistance to the chisels.

The laminating process enables the sculptor to carve woods that are only available in boards. Lamination opens to the carver a wide range of imported woods, while at the same time making possible a mixture of varied types and colors of wood into a single wood sculpture.

Teak, mahogany, and rosewood are some of the woods that can be carved by lamination if they are not available in logs. Coco bolo, lignum vitae, and ebony are just some of the exotic woods that are available in logs of sufficient volume to be carved. Usually these are available at sculpture supply stores or at lumber yards dealing in rare or imported woods. The sizes of imported logs are usually limited in volume; all are high in cost. The small volume and high cost of such logs combine to inhibit the spirit of adventure so necessary to explore the possibilities of direct carving.

The best wood to start with is a log available in your locale, no matter how rough that log may be. One of my favorite wood sculptures was carved from an old and gnarled oak tree that had been cut down and discarded in Yonkers, New York. City dumps also yield surprisingly good logs that are large in volume. Probably the most valuable log supply source for the woodcarver is the tree service company in your area.

Roots of trees are also good possibilities as carvable wood for the sculptor; they can be found at dumps, at landfills, and wherever land is being cleared.

The most prominent problem encountered by the student of woodcarving working with a log are what to do about the bark and the sapwood. The bark decays and tends to separate from the wood and fall off. If the sculptor wishes to include some bark in the finished work for special effect, this can be done by coating the bark to be included with two coats of polyurethane or shellac. Either solution is obtainable at any hardware store. Apart from such an exception, all bark should be removed before carving the wood.

In most woods, the sap is often of a different color than the wood. The sap is encountered under the bark. It is not uncommon for a log 12 inches in diameter to have a 2-inch-thick sap all around, leaving only an 8-inch diameter of wood. In such a case, if the sap is of a contrasting color to the wood, all sap should be removed before beginning the sculpture. Sharply contrasting colors of sap and wood can be distracting to the uniformity of the sculpture, although staining can eliminate this problem. However, the natural beauty of the wood cannot be improved by stains; for that reason, a decision should be made at the start whether to use or to exclude the sapwood of contrasting color. Some woods, such as maple or birch, have sap and wood of very similar color, which permits the sculptor to include both in the sculpture. Wood such as black walnut or red oak are of such natural beauty that staining would not be an improvement. Since both of these woods have sharply contrasting sap, all sapwood should be removed to ensure uniformity in the sculpture. A sculpture in black walnut with a few white bars or spots of sapwood left accidentally can spoil a good piece of work.

There are sculptors who use a hatchet or an adz to hasten the removal of bark and sap. However, I hesitate to use such tools or to recommend their use. The adz and the hatchet are not only hazardous to persons inexperienced in their use, but they are also not as sensitive as a woodcarving gouge. Removing bark and sap with a large wood-carving gouge with a blade width of from 1½ to 2 inches enables the sculptor to carve off the bark and sap while developing a rhythm of shapes on the wood.

Moving from the outside in, after the bark and sap, the next layers are the wood and, finally, the heartwood. The heartwood is the oldest wood in the log. The difference between wood and heartwood is not of much significance to the sculptor unless they are of different colors. For instance, in hickory, there is a sharp difference in color between the whitish wood and the deep brown heartwood, but in red oak there is no color difference at all between heartwood and wood. Deep undercuts that penetrate to the heartwood of a different color would reveal sudden color changes that can jar the unity of the form. Applewood also has a deeply colored heartwood and an off-white wood. When carving wood with contrasting colors, the carver can either choose a subject or a form that will lend itself to the color changes or plan to stain the finished piece. Finally, another option would be to split off all of the wood with splitting wedges and carve only the heartwood. I saw a well-carved head in hickory, but in every place where the carver penetrated into the heartwood, deep brown spots appeared in contrast to the whitish wood. One had the uncomfortable feeling of looking at a head that had been scalded. But again, a woman who carved bird forms and a man who carved free-form designs made excellent use of the two-toned wood. Ash has a slightly darker heartwood, but it is not contrasting enough to be offensive. Many heartwoods contrast gently and are complementary. Fortunately, most woods do not have contrasting colors between wood and heartwood.

special considerations
how to stop
cracking or checking

A special concern of the woodcarver is what to do about the cracking (checking) in green or unseasoned wood, especially since seasoned logs are almost nonexistent. The cracking is not as bad as it looks, but it can be disconcerting to the inexperienced carver.

The best of many solutions is the use of wax to seal the ends of the log before it is carved and also to fill all the cracks in the wood sculpture at the end of the carving process. Wood, especially freshly cut wood, is saturated with liquids, its own life fluids. These liquids or moisture begin to evaporate after a tree is cut. Evaporation of the moisture causes the wood to shrink, and the shrinkage causes cracking. Wood does not shrink lengthwise; it shrinks crosswise only, causing cracks to run from one end towards the next. Pure beeswax or brown petroleum wax are the waxes to use in arresting checks in wood. Brown petroleum wax is a special wax used by sculptors and jewelers as a modeling medium, as well as in the lost-wax casting process. Petroleum wax is obtainable at some art supply stores, at a foundry or casting, and at jewelers' supply dealers. Beeswax is obtainable at some hardware stores and artists' materials stores. Never use paraffin; it does not seal well enough for this purpose. The petroleum wax is very dark and would mar the unity of a sculpture in light-colored wood, such as maple; however, if petroleum wax is used to fill the cracks in a dark wood, such as walnut, it would blend very well. Use beeswax to fill cracks in light-colored woods.

When you obtain a log for carving, apply wax to both ends. The wax comes in rock-hard cakes and must be softened by heat before use. To prepare it, break off a few pieces with a hammer. For softening, place the pieces of wax in an old pot or tin can. Make sure that the tin can does not have a soldered bottom, or the solder will melt and discharge the very flammable wax. Wax is hard to control when in a liquid state. By adding water to the container that holds the wax and then allowing the water to heat (do not allow it to boil), the wax becomes mushy. When it is mushy, apply it with a painter's spackle knife to both ends of the log. The application of wax at the ends of the log seals the two main escape routes of evaporating moisture and forces the moisture to evaporate at a more moderate rate. This lessens the checking. The rapid evaporation of moisture from the end grain is the main reason for a sudden increase of cracking in the wood.

Hot wax is extremely flammable and explosive. The user of hot wax should never leave the heated wax unattended. Also, avoid holding your head directly over the top of the pot of wax while it is being heated. The water should never boil; water temperatures well below the boiling point are sufficient to soften wax. Remove the pot of wax from the heat when it is soft enough; replace it on the heat as needed. I have softened wax for use as a sealer by simply placing it under a slowly running hot water faucet. Use an electric hot plate for heating the wax. Never use a gas stove for this purpose. The flame from the stove will be a dangerous element.

Even after the ends of logs to be stored are waxed,

other cracks may appear during storage; fill these from time to time by pressing softened wax into the openings. Logs treated in this way will cure slowly and, if used many years later, will have dried evenly and will check less or hardly at all. This does not mean that a freshly cut log waxed on both ends should have to wait years to be carved. Green logs can be carved immediately, and wax may be used to stop the checks by filling cracks as they appear. Wood to be stored for later use should be stored out of doors if possible. If not, store it in the coolest place available. Heat accelerates checking by hastening moisture evaporation.

The waxed ends of the log should not inhibit carving—that is, if the nature of the sculpture demands that one or both waxed ends be carved away, then this should be done. The waxed ends are intended to slow down the cracking until carving time. Proceed with the sculpture even if new cracks appear. If any of the new cracks should be extra wide, fill them with wax. Otherwise, finish the sculpture and tolerate the cracks until the piece is complete—including the sanding, if intended.

To deal with cracks that open during the carving process, oil the sculpture with a mixture of linseed oil and turpentine, equal parts, or with any finishing oil or substance chosen. When the finishing oil is still present on the wood surface, press softened wax in all the cracks and then oil again. The presence of oil on the surface of the wood prevents the wax from sticking to areas where it is not wanted. A sculpture treated in this way will very rarely crack. Instead, from six months to a year later, the cracks will contract, squeezing out the wax. Wax is a long-lasting substance; any wax remaining in the wood will serve as a permanent seal against evaporating moisture. It is important to wax the bottom of the sculpture, if it has one—the portion of the wood on which the sculpture rests.

Very often, large, serious cracks in wood sculpture

are beyond the aid of wax, especially cracks approaching an inch wide or more. These are best filled with wedge-shaped slivers made from the same kind of wood or from any wood of a similar color. The wedges can be cut on a band saw or with a hatchet. Coat the wedges with Titebond or any other wood glue; then tap the wedges into the cracks, let them dry overnight, and chisel or saw the wedges until they are flush with the surface.

The term *cured wood* is something of a misnomer because of the nature of wood. Although curing means the removal of all moisture, there is nothing to prevent a kiln-dried board or log from absorbing moisture from the air and then reacting all over again to the evaporation of the new moisture it absorbed after it was cured. Wood reacts to atmospheric conditions.

Under natural conditions, a log of wood cures as slowly as about one-quarter inch per year from the outside in. Artificial methods of curing logs by exposing them to hot air are not widely available, and when they are, the logs cannot be large. Furthermore, they must be air-dried for a year before they can be successfully kiln-dried.

When all is said and done, the wax-sealing process seems to me to be the log carver's best answer, the key to controlling and stopping the cracking of wood.

I have seen some startling examples of the way wood reacts to temperature or to atmospheric changes. The wood sculptures of Ernst Barlach, the German sculptor, were brought from Germany to New York City for an exhibition. The wood sculptures were accustomed to the noncentral heating system of Germany before the 1950s. When the wood sculptures of Barlach were exposed to the central heating system in the United States, they protested as vigorously as anyone with a bad case of central heating sinus. The sculptures, which had previously stabilized, began to lose moisture rapidly in the hot, dry, central heating air. Cracks developed that turned insurance agents gray overnight. Lately, I visited an exhibition of Egyptian sculptures done centuries before the birth of Christ. One wood piece was cracking mightily with a half-inch crack straight down the middle. Clearly, the wood was reacting to the evaporation of moisture it had absorbed. It should have been sealed at the bottom with wax and perhaps with a coat of mat-drying polyurethane.

Pre-dried and laminated boards, when used for carving, eliminate the checking problem; so do kiln-dried logs. However, there is no substitute for the excitement gained from carving a rough, uncultured log—bark, sap, knots, cracks, and all. Each log has its own character.

woodcarving
tools

how to use the tools

ART supply or sculpture supply stores advertise dozens of types of woodcarving chisels and gouges in varied shapes and sizes. The existence of so many kinds of woodcarving tools is confusing to someone who has never carved wood. Although all kinds of woodcarving tools can be put to some use, most can be done without. Some designs, especially the very large gouges, 2 inches wide and over, are cumbersome.

Although I have bought dozens of beautifully designed woodcarving tools, I still use only a few basic tools to carve and model my wood sculptures. A lot of my tool purchases are responses to good-looking tool shapes, which I later discover to be inefficient.

Woodcarving tools are called chisels and gouges. Chisels are tools with flat blades, and gouges have U-curved cutting edges. The U-curve cutting edge of a gouge is called a "sweep." Numbers are used to describe the depth of the sweep in a gouge. A #11 sweep is almost a perfect U-shaped cutting edge, but a #4 sweep is so gentle a curve that it is almost a flat edge.

gouges

Gouges are described not only by their sweep but also by the shape of the shaft of the tool as it leaves the handle. A straight gouge is a gouge with a straight shaft; a short-bend gouge has a shaft that bends like a Sherlock Holmes pipe just before the cutting end. A long-bend gouge has a gently bending shaft. There are back-bend gouges, which bend opposite to the long bend—that is, they have a backward bending shaft. Gouges with bent shafts act as scoops when used. The shorter the bend, the sooner the gouge pops out of the wood (see Figure 7–1 for examples of tools).

A fish-tail gouge means what it says; it is a gouge with a blade that broadens at the edge like a fish's tail. A description of gouges in a tool suppliers' catalogue lists (1) "sweep" (the depth of the curve of

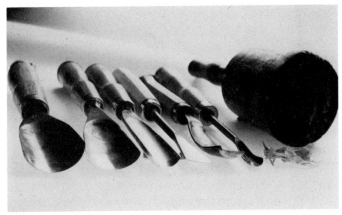

FIGURE 7-1 Woodcarving gouges and mallet. Left to right: 2-inch #9 sweep, 1 ¾-inch #7 sweep, 1-inch #9 sweep, fish tail, long-bend gouge, short-bend gouge, 2-pound, 4-inch diameter mallet. (Photo by Gordon Cruz)

the cutting edge). (2) "bend" (whether or not the shaft bends. is straight. or how it bends). and (3) width of cutting edge (see Figure 7-2).

A 1-inch gouge has a cutting edge 1 inch wide. A 1-inch #9 sweep gouge has a cutting edge 1 inch wide with a U-channel or sweep slightly less than a perfect "U." A 1-inch #9 straight gouge has all the above characteristics and has a straight shaft; but a 1-inch #9 sweep long-bend gouge has the same

FIGURE 7-2 Photo of tool showing the meaning of sweep and bend. (Photo by Gordon Cruz)

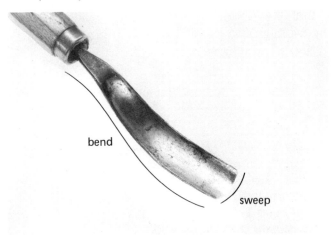

bend

sweep

measurements as the straight gouge, except that its shaft is bent like a lazy "S" or a smoker's pipe.

chisels Flat chisels are not as varied in shape as the gouges. The flat chisels are most effective as finishing tools. Flat woodcarvers' chisels are similar to a carpenter's flat chisel, but with a few added variations in design. Flat chisels are designed as their names suggest: They have flat cutting edges. Most are beveled on one side, but there is an exception called the "firmer" chisel, which is beveled on both sides. The main differences that I have found between a firmer chisel and a flat chisel with one side beveled are that the firmer chisel is more stocky and consequently more powerful, and because it is double-beveled, any side can face the wood. In single-beveled flats, the bevel must be against the wood for best results.

There are other flat chisel designs that are as superfluous as some of the gouge designs, but one important flat chisel for the woodcarver's use is the short-bend flat chisel. This is a flat chisel with an abrupt bend in the shaft. Its advantage when used is that it does not dig into the work as so many of the other designs tend to do.

A straight gouge with a numbered sweep can be used as a flat chisel because the sweep is so gentle that the gouge is almost flat, having a curve only slightly off a parallel line. This prevents it from digging in when used.

Below is a list of a good minimum number of tools for carving in wood:

1 *¾-inch (width of blade) #7 sweep straight gouge*
1 *1-inch (width of blade) #9 sweep straight gouge*
1 *½-inch (width of blade) #8 or 9 short-bend gouge*
1 *½-inch (width of blade) #7 sweep fish tail*
1 *Short-bend flat chisel, 1-inch blade*
1 *Heavy mallet, 2-pound weight*

A light mallet tires the arm. The best 2-pound mallet for the woodcarver is made of lignum vitae wood and is available at most good art supply stores. Mallets shaped like a judge's gavel will not do. Such a mallet produces the wrong kind of blow to the tool handle, causing the gouge to be driven like a nail. The striking body of a rounded mallet produces a better hitting stroke, and the sculptor need not aim, as with a hammer. After pauses, one has only to pick up the rounded mallet and use it without regard to its position. For close or delicate work, the mallet can be around its body and used for light tapping. The wooden handles of gouges and chisels are expendable. They split after some use. I have had handles last for years, but some last only a week. Attempts have been made by some manufacturers to produce longer lasting handles by placing a metal ring at the top of the handle. The metal prolongs the life of the inexpensive handle but destroys the precious and expensive wooden mallet. The problem is that with each blow of the mallet against the metal ring, a groove starts in the mallet that deepens and renders it useless. It is better to change handles when necessary, because the mallet can last a lifetime with care.

The best wooden handles are those reinforced with leather tops. When a chisel handle splits, or if it is worn from use, it is necessary to change the handle. New handles are available from the same source as the tools. Buy some extra handles when obtaining tools.

To change the handle, carefully chip away the handle by splitting off small portions with a flat carpenter's chisel. The tool should be resting flat on a work bench during the process. Do not try to pull the chisel out of the handle unless it is very loose. When the chisel is released from the handle, notice that the shank has four corners and that it tapers to a point. The shank is that part of the chisel that is sunk into the wooden handle. The corners of the shank are sharp enough to ream out the small predrilled hole on the newly obtained handle. Hold the new handle in one hand and the tool in the other. Place the shank into the hole in the handle and, with a wringing, twisting motion, enlarge the hole. Pause occasionally to tap out the wood dust from the hole. Take extra care to avoid touching the sharp blade during this process. Hold the tool high on the shaft. When the hole in the handle has opened enough to allow the shank to be pushed in, except for the last half-inch, place the edge of the chisel against the top of the work bench and tap it with the mallet until the last half-inch of the shank sinks into the handle. Bear in mind that the pre-drilled holes in the new handles are pilot holes; if chisels are forced in without enlarging the pilot hole, the handle will split immediately.

Another method that can be used to enlarge the pilot holes in new handles is to use an electric drill. A little bit of calculation is necessary for this method. The diameters of tool shanks vary with the size of the tools. If the base of the shank is ⅜-inch, tapering to a point, use a ¼-inch drill bit to widen the hole; then use a ⅜-inch drill bit to widen only the first ¾-inch. Next, insert the chisel. Making the hole wider at the beginning will help to accommodate the stouter base of the shank. The shanks are generally about 2½ inches long. The length of the shank determines the depth to which the pilot hole should be widened. Should a hole in the handle be too wide, allowing the tool to fall out, simply insert a wooden sliver or shim at the entrance of the hole and retap the chisel into the handle. Should a handle crack during use, the life of a cracked handle can be greatly extended by wrapping its entire length with electrical tape. Like a good hammerhead, the woodcarver's chisel can outlast many handles, or it can have one handle all its life.

using a gouge   To use the woodcarving gouge, grasp the tool by the handle and hold it in the palm. Hold it low on the handle with your hand toward the shank—

where the metal blade enters the wooden handle (see Figure 7–3). With a firm grasp, place the cutting edge against the wood at a steep angle, about 45°. Bring the mallet down to give the tool a whack. The sharp tool will enter the wood. Try this first cut near the top of a log standing on one end. A second whack and the gouge should start to travel; a third tap with the mallet and the tool should pop out with a mouthful of wood, leaving a score in its wake. The gouge does not have to be out of the wood in three strokes. The length of a cut with the straight gouge can be determined by manipulating the handle. Slight down pressure on the handle encourages the gouge to pop out; keeping a slight upward incline on the handle keeps the gouge in the wood. Long-bend and short-bend gouges will not take long cuts. Their designs are made for short scoops.

Which direction to cut in is a question. Assuming that the log is standing on one end, try cutting from

FIGURE 7–3 Hold the gouge low on the handle, with the hand toward the shank. (Photo by Gil McMillon)

left to right or right to left in a parallel line, or try the same cuts, moving the gouge slightly upward. Cut straight up near the top. Down strokes tend to split the wood, but they are good strokes after under-cuts have been made. The same down stroke that would split the material before any carving is done will become a stroke with the grain when it is used to move from high positive forms into valleys or negative spaces. Very often, the down stroke is the only nonsplitting cut feasible in an undercut. Gouge strokes need not run in one direction, nor do they have to be straight. Angle your gouge strokes and criss-cross them constantly. With enough practice, the gouge strokes can become an integral part of the sculpture because their pattern indicates the energy of the forms, and very often they reflect the sculptor's excitement during the carving process.

Avoid carving straight across the end of a log. A chisel traveling straight across the end grain of the wood can fracture and break. It is often necessary when making a sculpture from a log to carve at least one of its ends into a rounded rather than a flat shape. To reduce the flat top, start by gouging inward and upward from a point below the top, starting, say, 3 inches below the top but always cutting upward through the top, until the top of the log is rounded. It is generally thought that very large gouges are for removing much wood and speeding up the work, whereas small gouges are for finishing. But this is not true. Large gouges are slow. A gouge with a 1-inch width blade is a much faster tool than a 2-inch-wide gouge. The reason is that the larger the gouge, the more resistance it meets and the harder one must hit. The 1-inch #9 sweep slices through more readily. Using the same reasoning, when carving extremely hard wood or when carving the harder portions of a work, reduce the size of the gouge as resistance increases. A gouge does not have to take a full cut at each stroke; by rolling it over to one side, a smaller frac-tion of its width contacts the wood, so that a 1-inch gouge can be made to take a ¼-inch cut when necessary.

Long-bend gouges are good tools for cutting across the grains when modeling. Their design prevents them from sticking into the wood, as straight gouges tend to do. During crucial modeling stages, the long-bend gouge can enter and exit from a cut with two taps of the mallet without traveling into wood for a longer duration, fashioning hills and valleys, positive and negative planes with a dexterity denied the straight gouges. Short-bend gouges are essentially modeling tools. Short-bend gouges are not effective at the beginning stages of the carving, but they are essential for detailed work. Their design enables them to function like scoops. A half-inch wide short-bend gouge can be used to create short and sudden undercuts without affecting the surrounding material. Good taste should govern the use of short-bend gouges. Too often, they are overused, so that a wood carving is spoiled by being overwrought. I have omitted many tools from this discussion because so many tool designs are more fanciful than necessary. Bark-removing tools are unnecessary. The direct carving process removes the bark without making it a special effort requiring a special tool. In any case, tree bark does not cling tenaciously. Very large gouges, 1½ inches wide or more, can serve as bark removers. The large gouges are good tools for removing fussy gouge marks and also for making strong and simple undercuts. A good policy in buying large gouges is the following: The wider the blade, the more shallow the sweep or curve should be. An excellent large gouge is a 2-inch #7 sweep fish tail, or a 1¾-inch #8 sweep straight gouge.

Two groups of tools commonly confused with woodcarving tools are lathe-working tools and the printmaker's "wood-cut" tools used for block printing. Lathing tools are very rigid and are unsuitable for direct carving in wood. Tools designed for turning wood on a lathe are thick-bodied and cannot enter the wood in depth without splitting it. When buying woodcarving gouges, one can distinguish the difference between lathe tools and woodcarvers' tools by observing that the blade of the sculptor's gouge recedes in width as it moves towards the handle and shank but that the blade of the lathing tool has the same width from the cutting edge to the shank and handle.

The small tools designed for wood-cut methods are too fragile for woodcarving. The wood-cut or wood-engraving method requires that very shallow grooves be made in soft wood. But sculpture in wood requires the removal of large masses of wood as well as deep penetrations in, and often through, the wood, whether it is hard or soft. Wood-cut tools are designed to be pushed by hand, but woodcarving tools must be motivated with smacks from a heavy mallet. Because of the miniature scale of the tool, one can hardly hit a wood-cut tool with a mallet without hitting the hand. One way to distinguish between a wood-cut tool and a sculptor's gouge is that a standard wood-cut tool is about 4½ to 5 inches long, including the handle, but sculptor's gouges are at least 10 inches long with the handles, and some are 12 inches long, including handles.

When using the gouges, practice the difficult strokes instead of working only in the easy or convenient direction. The right-handed carver finds it convenient to work from right to left; the left-handed carver's easiest stroke is from left to right. But it is important in either case to practice the difficult strokes because the success of the sculpture requires chiseling in many directions, not just in one. I have found that by turning my back toward the wood, the difficult cross-stroke—in my case, from left to right—can be easily accomplished. The easy cross-cut is done facing the wood. The reason cutting in many directions is important is that if the chisel cuts are done in one direction only, the log will get smaller but will retain its original shape, somewhat like peeling an apple (the outer substance is removed, but the overall form remains the same). When gouge and chisel strokes move in many directions, a greater influence is exerted on the wood, and new shapes develop sooner. The cross-stroke, across the grain, helps to flatten the sausagelike roundness of the log. The up-and-down stroke breaks up the stiltlike vertical planes in which the tree grew.

Practice the good habit of marking with chalk on the wood to denote the line from which to carve. Carving away with no reference point is aimless and contributes to soft and pointless forms. In the absence of firm markings clearly indicating your intentions, aims can be forgotten between pauses, and precious volume can be lost.

It is best to cut in a direction that moves away from the line, since the line made indicates the point from which to cut. The point is that a line made on the sculpture being carved indicates the point from which the sculptor wishes to remove materials, so that the line eventually becomes an outline against space.

Experiment and discover tool uses. Notice that the grains of wood change radically at knots, branch ends, and burls. Respond to what is happening at the moment. If you are carving in one direction and the wood suddenly splits, change the direction of the chisel stroke to whatever the wood allows without splitting. Splitting is an indication that the chisel stroke is against the grain. Splitting should not be confused with shredding. It is normal for the wood surface to shred from cuts across the grain—that is, after a cut across the grain, the surface is rough-edged. Such rough edges are smoothed in the finishing process, so they should be tolerated during the carving. Splitting is a different matter. When the gouge is run against the grain, one can hear the split and see that a large piece of wood is being ripped. A great deal of risk is also involved in breaking the chisel during splitting.

As the sculpture moves towards its finish, use gouges with shallow rather than deep sweeps. When deep-sweep gouges are employed too close to the finishing stages, they gouge too deeply, devouring precious volume. After using the gouges that are very shallow in sweep, the flat chisels are next to be used in the finishing process.

using a chisel or flat

The chisel should be thought of as the finishing tool. If a sculpture in wood is to be finished with all tool marks visible, chisels are unnecessary. Even if the sculpture is to be smoothed so that gouge marks disappear, this can be done with a rasp, therefore bypassing the flat chisels. However, chisels are more sensitive tools than rasps, and it is good practice to apply flat chisels to areas where smooth surfaces are required or even to areas where gouge marks are desired in lower relief. The rasp files down the gouge marks while changing the forms at random, but the chisel removes the gouge marks while refining, even improving, the existing forms.

I shall list the chisels important to the sculptor, deliberately omitting those that are unnecessary.

The firmer chisel is a flat chisel that is beveled on both sides. The skew chisel is a flat chisel with one corner recessed. The short-bend flat chisel is a chisel with a spoonlike bend at the end of the shaft. A carpenter's bench chisel beveled on one side is a valuable sculptor's chisel.

The firmer chisel beveled on both sides is useful in reducing gouge grooves to a level surface while retaining or improving the integrity of the forms being carved. The skew chisel with its recessed edge allows scraping and finishing in crevices and recesses. Its slanted cutting edge is offered less resistance by the wood, and therefore it can "dig in" or split the wood.

A good chisel is the short-bend flat chisel. The sharply bent shaft of this chisel prevents it from jabbing into the wood when it is used. It takes short, clean cuts, which makes it an excellent tool for finishing. Flat chisels need not be dealt hard blows with the mallet. They are not removers of wood; rather, they should be considered as scrapers and shavers. Flat chisels should be used as much as possible with the grain of the wood. A well-sharpened flat chisel can be pushed by hand for very delicate surface work (see Figure 7–4 for examples of tools).

Vary the tools used during the carving process. This practice adds variety to the surface texture. Remember that straight gouges—not flat chisels— are the main tools to use in blocking out the work. A common occurrence with students of woodcarving is to drive the chisel or gouge up to the hilt into the wood. When this happens, the tool is stuck and cannot be pulled out. Prying it by the handle can break the steel. The best method of extricating an embedded tool is to chip away all the wood above

FIGURE 7–4   Chisels. Left: a gouge of very shallow sweep, usable as a flat chisel; center: a short-bend chisel; right: a carpenter's flat chisel, beveled on one side only. (Photo by Gordon Cruz)

the stuck tool until it falls out or can be easily removed. If a chisel starts to dig in, stop, pull it out and change the direction of the cut.

In summarizing about woodcarving tools and their uses, it can be said that the quality of the steel is important to the quality and strength of the tool. The sculptor has no way of judging the quality of the steel, but by buying tools that are sold and made by reputable companies, he or she is assured that the product is reasonably good. Do not buy carving tools from hobby shops. Very large tools look good in the studio, but they are not of much use. When buying gouges for practical purposes, stay with those that have blade widths under 1½ inches. The gouges and the chisels can become an extension of the mind and hands, not just tools for removing surplus wood. The process of wood sculpture is very enjoyable, sometimes even more enjoyable than the finishing. But always, the enjoyment of the process is evident in the finished sculpture.

how to sharpen woodcarving tools

KNOW WHAT YOU'RE
READING ABOUT, BEFORE
YOU EVEN ATTEMPT TO
BELIEVE ½ of THIS.
READ - LEE VALLEY GUIDE
TO SHARPENING
INSTEAD.

For many years, when I lived in New York City, I avoided confronting the delicate art of sharpening woodcarving tools by simply returning them to Sculpture Associates, where I'd bought them, and paying a fee for sharpening. I would use a hand-held slipstone to keep them keen, but as soon as they needed serious grinding, I would take them to the professional tool sharpeners. This was a comfortable practice until later, when I moved to a small town in southern Vermont where no one had ever heard of a sculptor, much less of sculpture-tool sharpening. The closest I could come to a tool sharpener was the local chainsaw-sharpening shop. Since woodcarving tools require a much different sharpening technique than a chainsaw blade, I was forced to sharpen my own tools; although the process was painful at first, it was useful in the end.

However, the idea of using the services of a professional tool sharpener is a good one, especially if it is inexpensive and if the sculptor dislikes tedium with the same intensity that I do. But one can go too far the other way, too. When I began to teach, I was surprised to discover that there are people who love to sharpen tools, to such an extent that a tool capable of lasting a lifetime of use is ground away to zero in a month. Avoid oversharpening. Sharp enough is sharp enough.

Woodcarving tools are sold unsharpened, unless sharpening is requested by the buyer. Not all dealers have a sharpening service. For this reason, a beginning carver should ascertain whether or not carving tools are available sharpened or unsharpened, thus anticipating a sharpening problem at the very start. The bigger the dealer, the more likelihood there is that sharpening the tools is part of the service. On the other hand, if there is a general tool-sharpening shop in your locality, then such a place can help the beginner with the sharpening of new tools. A well-sharpened tool can be used for a month on hard wood without the need to sharpen it. The same tool, if mishandled, or if it encounters tough end-grain, branch butts, or knots, can require sharpening after such encounters.

The blades of sharpened tools are delicate and can be nicked if they are knocked against each other or hard surfaces. Protect sharpened tools by wrapping the blades with paper when transporting them, or carry them in a cloth pouch designed for such purposes. Tool knapsacks are available at hardware stores.

While you are beginning to learn how to sharpen, use a hand-held slip stone. A slip stone is a honing or sharpening stone and is very effective and fast. Slip stones vary in shape and composition. Some are called Arkansas stones, and other kinds are called India stones: Both are artificial. Some India slip stones contain aluminum oxide abrasives. There are numerous artificial abrasives included in the composition of artificial stones, but their characteristics are not important to the user. The most practical slip stone shapes are the conical and the wedge-shaped slip stones. The conical slip stone is curved to fit the sweep of the gouges; thus, it makes total contact with the cutting edge when used. These stones are particularly effective in removing jagged edges or burrs from the inner surface of the blade. Whenever a tool is sharpened, the inner edge of the blade becomes lined with a fragile burr. The wedge-shaped slip stone is useful in removing the burr from the inner surface of small tools (see Figure 7–5).

Oil is the traditional agent used to lubricate whetting stones, but I prefer water. Oil clogs the stone's grit and dulls its abrasiveness.

Since the conical slip stone imitates the shape of the gouges, it also tapers from about 2 inches wide and downward to about a half an inch. This tapering allows it to fit a wide range of different sizes of gouges. The gouge has a hollow interior and a

FIGURE 7–5 A burr, or roughness, develops on the inner edge of the tool after sharpening. The roughness can be smoothed by using a slip stone or by pushing the tool against the corner of the bench stone, rotating the inner edge until all is smoothed. (Photo by Gordon Cruz)

bulging exterior blade—like a U and so does the conical slip stone.

To use the slip stone, hold it in one hand, hollow side up. Place the gouge, hollow side up, into the slip stone (they will fit like hand and glove). Keep the tool handle high enough to bring the bevel and the cutting edge of the tool into contact with the stone. After about six pushes of the tool, stop. Test the edge of the gouge by pushing it against wood. If it needs to be sharper, repeat the above. When the edge of the tool is sharp enough, reverse the slip stone and reverse the gouge so that the inner curve of the gouge fits the outer bulge of the stone. In this position, the inner edge of the tool can be sharpened.

When using the wedge-shaped slip stone, hold the tool in one hand and the stone in the other and move the dampened slip stone against the tool's edge. When the stone is pushed from the edge of the blade toward the handle, it cuts faster than when using the reverse motion. Use the stroke to fit the intent. The slim body of the wedge-shaped slip will fit into tools ½ inch wide or less. It's a good practice, while pausing to observe the work, to use a slip stone to make the edge of the tool keen. A very effective and simple way to sharpen is with the bench stone, so-called because it can be used while it rests on the work table. Bench stones are usually made of carborundum. The stone in Figure 7–5 measures 6 inches long, 2 inches broad, and 2 inches thick. A strip of 2" x 4" is nailed to the work bench to prevent the stone from sliding, and water is poured on for lubrication (Figure 7–6).

Before sharpening a tool, observe its shape. The aim in sharpening should be to maintain the original shape of the cutting edge and a straight bevel. The bevel is usually about ¼ inch above the edge of the blade. As sharpening and resharpening occurs, the distance between bevel and edge shortens. It is then necessary to move back the bevel.

FIGURE 7–6 A strip of 2″ × 4″ is nailed to the workbench to prevent the stone from sliding. Water is poured on for lubrication. (Photo by Gordon Cruz)

Although power sanders are used for moving back bevels, the bench stone can do this without the danger of burning the steel through the friction of grinding. The gouge in Figure 7–5 needed a new bevel line. To do this, place the gouge on the bench stone, holding the handle at an angle that brings the bevel line into contact with the stone. The rest of the gouge should be out of contact with the stone. The gouge is semi-circular; therefore, the only way to bring the entire edge of its blade into contact with the whetting stone is to roll the gouge from the extreme left to the extreme right as it is pushed forward along the stone's surface (see Figures 7–7 and 7–8). The fingers are in the channel of the tool applying much pressure. The gouge being sharpened is a straight gouge of ¾-inch width and #8 sweep.

The bench stone method of sharpening is a worthwhile method for the woodcarver to master because it involves no machinery and because there is no risk of damaging the tool through the heat produced by friction, as is the case when using power equipment. Bench-stone sharpening is, of

FIGURE 7–7 The only way to bring the entire blade into even contact with the whetting stone is to roll the tool from the extreme left to the extreme right as it is pushed forward along the stone's surface. (Photo by Gordon Cruz)

FIGURE 7–8 The gouge has traveled halfway along the length of the bench stone and has been rolled from one side to the center. A steady control is kept on the angle that keeps the distance from bevel to edge at a consistent pitch. (Photo by Gordon Cruz)

course, slow. Pass after pass has to be made before the gouge is successfully sharpened. The main aim is to recreate or maintain a straight bevel and a clean pitch from bevel to edge (see Figure 7–9). Bench stones can be artificially made or composed of two different textures, or they can be natural sandstone. Any kind of bench stone does the job. It is hard to offer any specific preference.

Hand-turned or electric-powered emery wheels are unsuitable for sharpening woodcarving tools. The

FIGURE 7–9 The sharpening stroke is completed, and the gouge has been rotated to the side opposite from the starting point. The motion is repeated until the edge is keen and a clean, clear bevel is created or maintained. A new bevel is only required if the distance from bevel to edge becomes very narrow, well under ¼ inch. (Photo by Gordon Cruz)

main problem is that the breadth of the wheel is too narrow to accommodate the average wood tool. And the emery invariably becomes bumpy. The very best sharpening wheel for woodcarving tools is the solid sandstone wheel of antiquity. Some woodworking tool suppliers offer such a wheel. Usually large, such sandstone wheels are about 2½ feet in diameter and 4 inches wide. Some are hand-cranked and some are pedal-driven. All such stones must be kept wet when used. With luck, one can find such stones for sale at a county fair or flea market.

The very best electric-powered sharpening system is one that drives sanding belts. The sanding belts are of aluminum oxide or carbide and do a rapid job of reconditioning tools. Again, the tool must be constantly dipped in water in order to prevent heating and burning of the precious metal. The electric-powered, sanding-belt tool sharpener is expensive and is more suited for use in a studio with many persons. An individual sculptor can do very well with the manually operated sharpening stones.

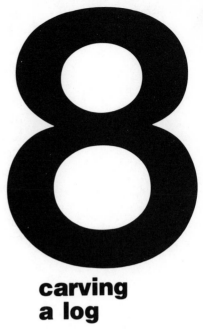

8

**carving
a log**

THE availability of logs for carving varies according to one's location. I have a sculptor friend who lived in New York and Vermont and carved wood and stone, eventually favoring wood as the major carving material. My friend moved to a town in California and discovered an absence of available wood or stone for carving in that particular town. This does not mean that there is no wood or stone in California, but it demonstrates that the availability of these materials can change from region to region. When logs are unavailable for carving, planks or boards can be glued together to form a suitable carving stock. If one is lucky enough to be living in an area where logs of wood are abundant, then tremendous explorations into the art of woodcarving from logs can be practiced. No two logs are alike, and the difference between each log encourages variety in the woodcarver's art. Be cautious when taking form suggestions from the log as it is found, because once carving begins, the original outlines of the log are bypassed by the process of subtraction.

the carving process
working with a log

First-time woodcarvers are inclined to choose a small piece of wood for their first attempt at woodcarving. Actually, a medium-sized piece of wood, or even a large log, is better for the beginner than a small-sized bit of wood. Larger logs are stable enough by their own weight to allow carving without having to brace or clamp the wood in order to prevent it from falling every time it is jarred by the chisel strokes. The larger logs have a sufficient volume to allow experiments and trials and errors. A log of wood 6 inches in diameter and 12 inches long can be considered small. A 3- to 4-foot-high log, 10 to 12 inches in diameter or more, is a good size for a first attempt at carving wood. Such a log has enough volume to allow the beginner to change his or her plans and to experiment as he or she gains understanding.

A log may be halved before carving. Half a log,

split lengthwise, is not only an interesting shape to start with, but it will also cut the possibilities of checking. Most tensions that cause cracking happen in the central parts of the log. Splitting the log not only exposes the middle to air; it also separates the center where pressure and movement cause the checks.

It is possible to split logs over 4 feet in height. The log does not have to be split equally, and one half can be expendable, which allows the gradual chipping away of one half in order to save the other for the sculpture. A heavy sledge and two wood-splitting wedges are all the tools needed to split the log. Drive one wedge into the wood at the spot where the splitting is desired. Hammer the wedge in halfway, then place the next wedge in alongside the first, and hammer it in halfway with heavy blows of the sledge. A crack should appear. Remove the wedges and repeat the process until the wood splits off. Do not drive the wedges all the way in because removing them for renewed wedging will then be difficult. Continue to split off portions until half of the log is left intact. Sometimes a log can be split in two halves at one stroke in the center with a wedge and sledge or with an axe.

The carving table upon which the wood is mounted must be sturdy. Tables designed for use as furniture are seldom stable enough to serve as woodcarving benches; however, junk shops sometimes have sturdy tables designed by factories or machine shops that can serve as woodcarvers' tables. Very little skill is required to make a sturdy woodcarving table. The legs should be made of 4" x 4" planks: Pine or fir will do. Brace the legs with 2" x 4" boards, also of pine or fir. Plyboard ½ inch thick is adequate for the top, which need not exceed 2½ to 3 feet square. How high the table should be is determined by the length of the log to be carved. Very tall logs are more conveniently carved on a low table or on no table at all, assuming that the log is stood on one end while being carved. Short logs are more comfortably carved on high tables. The aim in determining the proper table height is to have the top of the log to be carved about even with eye level when the log is standing on one end, assuming that the sculptor is also standing.

A standing position is the best for carving. It is difficult to swing a 2-pound mallet while seated, and a better understanding of the work is gained if the sculptor can move around the piece constantly. But all of this does not mean that there are any rules against carving while seated or even against carving without a table. The sculptor should adopt the method that feels most comfortable or that is best suited for the work to be done. If a log of wood is 9 feet high, then, clearly, it does not need a table. If the log to be carved is unstable, whether large or small, it can be made stable enough to prevent it from rocking when it is struck with a mallet and chisel by supplying it with a plyboard base or footing. The base must form a square larger in area than the diameter of the end of the log it must stabilize. If the diameter of the log is 12 inches, then supply it with a base 2 feet square. Use four 2-inch-long nails to attach the plyboard to the bottom of the log; then, after the plyboard has been firmly nailed to the log, nail the four corners of the plyboard footing to the work table. The wood can then be carved without having it fall or move at each stroke from the mallet and chisel.

With the log standing on one end, carving with the gouge moving from left to right or right to left, in parallel strokes, is carving across the grain. Straight-up gouge strokes are with the grain; so are straight-down strokes. The downstroke should be avoided until undercuts are made. When the wood is a flat vertical surface from top to bottom, the downstroke tends to split it, but this stroke works well after the wood has been indented. A good way to start the sculpture is to taper the flat top and grain of the log by carving upward and by working all around at the top until the flat end becomes rounded or domelike. This exercise allows the beginner to force the wood to yield some of its volume. As flattened areas become round, the sculptor may see a suggestion of an image.

exploring the subject

Before attempting to create a direct carving of any subject, it is important to be knowledgeable of or familiar with the shapes and design of the subject to be carved. Study the subject, draw it, look at it, and make any observations needed to carve it successfully, such as which parts are furthest out and which furthest in. Carving a subject that is unfamiliar is not a feasible undertaking. In case photographs are used as the major source of reference for the subject, make allowance for the fact that the photographs cannot show the three-dimensional relationships between the planes. For example, a photograph of the human head, front view, does not inform us that the relationship between the ear on the left and the ear on the right is not a flat line, but a full half-circle. If you own a camera, make your own photographic observations of many angles of the subject of your interest.

Carving from a log can also be done by simply venturing to subtract wood without having any specific plan. Most of the creativity in carving happens after the sculpture starts. Do not look for total clarity at the beginning of a wood carving, but instead, interpret the new shapes as they are revealed by the subtraction of wood with the gouges, and then make decisions based on visual observations.

Another approach toward solving the problem of "what to carve" is to make a few drawings of ideas on paper. The drawings should conform as much as possible to the general shape of the wood to be carved. The sculpture cannot be expected to copy the drawing exactly. Draw one or more views and let the sculpture discover the unresolved views. Pin the drawings on a wall nearby for easy reference. This last method of approach to carving is very helpful to persons who work best when working from a plan. The most helpful drawing from which to start the sculpture is a drawing of a profile or side view of the subject. A side view immediately shows the carver where all of the most important center high points are and how the masses at the center relate to each other. The profile drawing serves to remind the sculptor that in a three-dimensional form, all of the planes are not visible from any one view. As I have said in earlier chapters, the outlines constantly change as the sculpture develops. Reluctance to change outlines hampers the growth and progress of the sculpture.

Remember that the dynamics of a wood carving depend upon exploiting the interior volumes of the log of wood. Students of carving always tell me that there is not enough room in the wood for that 7-inch projection, but the truth is that a 7-inch subtraction must happen in order to produce a bulge of equal measure. Find all of the volumes of the design by carving in; the process of slow subtraction of the material reveals the presence of the forms being sought. With the importance of the center of the design firmly in mind, look at the profile drawing of your plan. Draw a firm center line on the wood to indicate where you wish to have the center of your sculpture; then begin to carve sharply away from both sides of the line, making sure that the gouge digs in deeper as it moves away from the line. This starts the sculpture and causes the center line to be higher than the other planes, which is as it should be. Later, other sketches can be made to point the way for other profiles of the design as they evolve, and if no clue as to their forms is given by the materials. Keep an open mind and adjust the original concept, if needed, in order to seize opportunities that may arise by pure chance. Very often, after the sculpture has progressed past the first stages, the sculptor may have a complete change of mind regarding the first concept in favor of a better idea. If you change your mind about the first plan in favor of a new one, it is safe to abandon the first for the new, because shapes left by the cancelled plan can be adjusted to fit the new idea. Some of my best sculptures in wood started out with one idea and were changed to exploit shapes that developed while carving. Usually, such accidental discoveries are more compatible to the material, since the forms were visually suggested by it and were therefore present.

Give the wood sculpture enough time to grow. Do not try for too rapid results. In three-dimensional carving, all of the parts are interrelated, so that no one section can be totally seen until its relatives are developed. This point is important, because too often, a student of carving may try for days to resolve one section of a piece without realizing that it cannot be resolved until all of the other components of the whole design are developed.

To demonstrate carving a log, I decided to carve *Majestic Eagle* in black walnut. To make the sculpture powerful enough to convey the idea of the power of the eagle, I thought it should be large enough to relate to human scale without being diminutive. I obtained the log from the local tree service, always my favorite wood supply source. The huge walnut log measured 6 feet by 6 inches and was 3 feet in diameter at its broadest section. I used a most direct approach to carving this log. No drawings or plans were made. I knew I wanted to carve an eagle, but in what attitude, I left open. I spent a good deal of time looking at eagles at the zoo, both live and stuffed. Although this was not my first sculpture of an eagle, I have always had to study any subject over again every time it is to be carved. I decided that when the eagle flies, its wings are the dominant shapes, but when it is standing, as the sculpture would present it, then the head is the most important part of the creature's elegant apperance. Next came its attitude, or posture. I wanted the majestic eagle to look like its

**carving
"majestic eagle"**

title—aloof—and finally the clawed feet must complete the portrait. By portraying the eagle's clawed feet as part of its portrait, I hope to present this sculpture of an eagle as it must look in the eyes of its prey, which must hold the eagle's talons in awe.

For tools, I chose a 1-inch-wide #9 sweep straight gouge as the largest tool because walnut is hard wood, and therefore smaller tools are best. Two other gouges were chosen, a ¾-inch-wide #7 sweep straight gouge, and a short-bend ⅜-inch-wide gouge for deep and detailed modeling. The mallet I chose was 2 pounds in weight.

The first thing I tackled was the flat 2½-foot-wide top of the log. The eagle's head was to be extracted from the top, and the flatness had to be rounded at once. By using strong upstrokes, I sloped the wood at the top all around until it formed an elongated dome. Frequent cross-strokes were used to "flatten" the cylindrical shape of the log. The effort to change the top from a flat surface to a dome required two days.

It is important when carving to stick to the aim you have decided on. The time spent ridding the wood of its flat top was not experienced as a labor; to the contrary, it was stimulating and instructive because, during the process, my imagination began to conjure up the eagle's head. Which way should it be turned? How large should it be? Almost each hour that passed, my plans for the head changed, re-formed, and changed again; during all this, the carving effort continued to confine itself strictly to rounding out the top. By the time the top was rounded, I knew where to place the eagle's head and which way it should be turned. The head was the first form sought, but it was not to be finished until all of the rest of the eagle had been completed. The photograph of the early stages of the sculpture in black walnut of *Majestic Eagle* shows that the flat top of the log, which became a sloping dome, enabled me to fashion the eagle's head

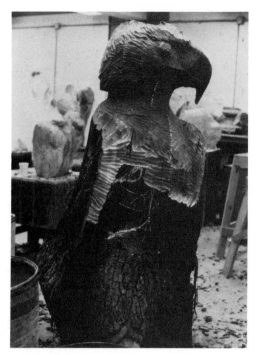

FIGURE 8–1 The early stages of *Majestic Eagle*. The head was hewn out of the top end grain.

FIGURE 8–2 The head in profile. The chalkline on the neck and breast of the eagle mark the center high point. The wood is being carved away and in from the line. Much of the log remains uncarved in this early stage and still retains its bark.

from the top end grain. Chalk marks denote the high points from which to carve inward (see Figure 8–1).

Although the head and neck are cleared from the rest of the wood, I still must wait for further carving before making decisions about all of the rest of the sculpture (see Figure 8–2). After the beak and the head of the eagle were cleared, I shifted the position of the breast so that instead of aligning itself with the front of the eagle's beak, the front of the breast is at right angles to the front of the beak. This shift causes the sculptured eagle to look sharply to its left. This was not a predicted shift in the forms, but the decision was made at a moment during the carving because a rhythm in the wood suggested it. I pursued this method of unplanned carving during the carving of this piece. Of course, details and modeling are planned; what is discovered is the relationship between the parts. I enjoy the surprises in store within the uncarved wood, and I am reluctant to miss the surprises by planning a sculpture out in advance. No mistakes can be made, because no plans have been made. This is a good system for the beginner to try. It permits experiments.

The sculpture progressed from the top down, as can be seen in Figure 8–3. One folded wing is being popped out purely by subtraction and also by stopping that subtraction at the points along which I want to show the folded wing. Notice that, on the left, no wing has appeared as yet. To create a wing at the left, I will simply carve deeper, from center to wing, stopping short of the wing. This technique is, in essence, how direct carving works. Projections reflect depressions.

FIGURE 8–3 At this stage, the sculpture could no longer progress unless the whole figure was blocked out—from head to breast to legs and feet. (Photo by Gil McMillon)

At the stage shown in Figure 8–3, the sculpture could no longer progress unless the whole figure was roughed out—from head to breast to legs to feet. The basic relationships between the masses of an eagle standing are that the tip of the beak is furthest out, next the breast, and then the feet. This means a rapid descent from beak to breast and then from breast to feet. I started the sculpture with a log that was absolutely vertical from top to bottom. To express the descents from head to breast to feet required deep and bold undercuts. The relationships between the eagle's beak and breast and between the breast and the legs are rapidly descending ones, calling for strong undercuts (see Figure 8–4). In order to express the suddenness of these rapidly varying planes, the undercuts would have to eliminate huge chunks of wood. It is important for the sculptor to be able to make portions of the material expendable in order to create the relationships between the masses of a form. The quantity of wood to be subtracted cannot be removed mechanically by sawing because the undercut

FIGURE 8–4 Here, it can be clearly seen that projections in a direct carving are obtained by subtractions. The extent of the projections is precisely equal to the depth of the subtractions, or undercuts. (Photo by Chee Heng Yeong)

moves into the wood in an unpredictable way. The crucial point is that the removal process describes and discovers all of the shapes that are being created. Cutting in with a saw, in an attempt to quicken the process, often swipes off much of the wood needed for the proper transition between planes. All of the forms in a sculpture are related to each other, so that when carving in any one area proceeds, the carving moves straight into the next neighboring area. It can be clearly seen in Figure 8–4 that strong undercuts produce forceful bulges. Notice that the wood subtracted at the top of the sculpture (see the arrow at the top of Figure 8–4) caused the breast to protrude. The deep undercut below the breast (see the arrow at the bottom in Figure 8–4) completed the description of the full bulge of the breast.

Any direct carving in wood depends upon undercuts (such as those seen in Figure 8–4) for definition of the shapes and, indeed, for the modeling of details. By glancing at Figure 8–3 and then turning to Figure 8–4, the reader can see the strength of the undercut that had to be made below the breast in order to create the full round form that constitutes the breast of the sculpture of *Majestic Eagle*. The compensation for boldly probing into the wood is the discovery of new and hidden forms. Undercutting below the eagle's breast revealed the first suggestion of the thigh. The bottom arrow in Figure 8–4 points to the thigh in its early stage of discovery. The tip of the beak in *Majestic Eagle* extends to the original exterior surface of the wood, but the throat was created after a 12-inch undercut (see the arrow in Figure 8–5). The vertical line flanking the sculpture roughly defines the original exterior of the wood. Early details can be seen in the head. A short-bend gouge ½-inch wide was my detail tool. The idea is to stroke the wood in the direction one wants the forms to move in. Around the eye, swirling motions. Atop the head, the upward movement of feather shapes. On the breast, a slanted upward movement to the left and right of

FIGURE 8-5 The tip of the beak in *Majestic Eagle* extends to the original exterior of the wood, but the throat was created after a 12-inch undercut, marked here by the arrow. (Photo by Chee Heng Yeong)

center. As carving progressed on the breast to the left and right of the center high point, the folded wings of the eagle began to protrude. Again, this is an exercise of raising protrusions by subtracting into the depressions. This was the system used to raise the folded wing visible in Figure 8–5.

I employed the "stop-cut" method to raise the wing; the expression literally means "stop the cut." I drew a line where I wished the folded wing to appear, carved downward toward the line, and stopped at the line. When this was done down to a depth of 6 inches, the folded wing protruded outward to the same measurement. It is natural to experience qualms over using bold undercuts, especially for the first-time woodcarver. One way of getting bold about undercutting is to do it in stages—a little at a time. Start with a shallow undercut, observe it, and then deepen it. Use the cut-in-and-stop method for undercutting. Drive the gouge in with two hits from the mallet; then extricate the gouge. Then repeat another two hits, and the gouge can bite straight in for a few inches in just four well-directed mallet hits. The undercut below the beak of *Majestic Eagle* in Figure 8–5 did not happen in a direct way. From the exterior of the wood, I had to penetrate about 12 inches deep to the eagle's throat. But that depth could not be predicted; it could have been less or more. Simultaneously with carving in from the front, I carved downward from the top on both sides of the head. Finally, as the head and beak became clearly carved, and as I carved both sides of the beak, a small hole appeared as a gouge stroke broke through. This first breakthrough was then enlarged to separate the beak tip from the rest of the wood. Negative spaces discovered in this way are most compatible to the surrounding positive forms they complement and with the forms that they undercut.

Walnut is a hard wood with very grained or layered properties. Carving across the grains exposed a shredded surface. The shredding is a natural result of cross-grain carving and should be tolerated. The finishing carving strokes with the grains will correct this. *Majestic Eagle,* after more than four months of steady carving, was now ready for the finishing stages, which require strong suggestions of feet at the base and with-the-grain chiseling to correct the frayed edges caused by cross-grain carving strokes. Gouge marks were left throughout the work. I felt that the sculpture would have more vitality, in this case, if left rough-hewn (see Figures 8–6 and 8–7).

from static log to "torso in motion"

A simple, straight log of wood can be made to yield a form that has more movement than the log from which it was carved. Too often, students of carving seek out logs that have bends and curves in order to carve sculpture with motion. But it is actually better to create your own motion by the process of carving while applying your own designs. As so often happens, a log that already has a strong rhythm cannot be made to assume a different form. The result is that the sculptor working with such a

FIGURE 8–6 The sculpture finished in the rough. (Photo by Chee Heng Yeong)

FIGURE 8–7 Close-up of the head showing the details enhanced by tool marks. (Photo by Chee Heng Yeong)

log ends up yielding to the log's shape, which in turn produces a sculpture from a log that looks like a log.

In carving a log of regular shape, I plan to cause it to take on motion—the motions of a torso of the human figure. By placing a few lines on the wood indicating the main guides to the motions I have in mind and then by carving away from these lines, which are the main motivators of the sculpture, I hope to show in stages that the direct carver need not find a log already in motion in order to create movement in a sculpture in wood. With no preliminary drawings, but with a firm chalkline down the center representing the middle front of the torso, a downward slanting line at the top indicates my intentions to slope one shoulder down; and with an opposing upward slanting line at the lower part of the sculpture, I hope to place the hips—one raised, one lowered—to conform to the movements of a torso in this particular stance. All of this is seen in Figure 8–8. The log measures 3½ feet high, and 1 foot 3 inches in diameter. At the moment, the chalklines mark my intentions. To change intentions into actuality, I must carve away from the outlines. The center line is the place from which to start the carving. The reason for starting at the center is that it is to become the highest plane—the profile line—and carving directly must move from high planes to middle and low planes.

The carving stroke moves to the left and to the right from the center. As the gouge moves away

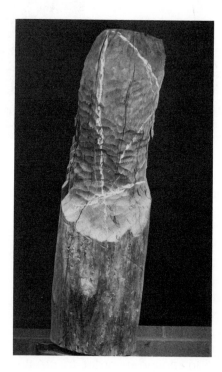

FIGURE 8–8 The vertical chalkline at the center marks the central high point of the torso and the most important point of the structure of the sculpture. (Photo by Chee Heng Yeong)

from its starting point at the center, the cut becomes deeper. This technique of carving deeper towards the end of the cut ensures that the carving stroke is moving into the wood. Carving strokes traveling across the wood remove material evenly but change nothing. Cuts that make no changes are in order during the finishing process but waste needed material at the blocking-out stages of the sculpture. As the carving moves inward, the forms pop outward. To create a downward sloping shoulder, the wood mass above the chalkline at the top in Figure 8–8 will be cut back at the line. The movement of the shoulder emerges as the wood is slowly cut back at the line. Through drawing and modeling in clay, I've studied the human figure, yet each time I use it in carving, I have found it necessary to renew my observations by making new drawings from a model. Notice that the end grain at the top has been sloped back and rounded so that the top and the sides have literally merged to become one plane. The upstroke was used to merge the top and the sides. This upward sloping movement allowed me to slope the center line of the torso so that some movement began. If the log is to be changed into a sculpture with motion, the vertical plane of the log, from top to bottom, should be the focus of a concentrated effort to curve its original straightness. Whenever this vertical plane of the log is allowed to prevail throughout the sculpture, then the end result is a treelike sculpture. Deep undercuts into the log change its treelike shape and produce movement in the sculpture. Movement was created in the sculpture of *Torso in Motion* by curving the center line (see Figure 8–9). The center line disappears from view toward the bottom because it is shifted off center, thus creating movement. Notice in Figure 8–8 that the chalk lines clearly indicate the edges from which the wood has been carved—the edges of the planes of the figure. Cuttings must go very sharply in to create the turnings of the planes. This is what creates the light and shade on the sculpture and gives

FIGURE 8–9 Movement was created in the sculpture of *Torso in Motion* by curving the center line. (Photo by Chee Heng Yeong)

it definition. Knowing where to place the lines denoting the planes depends on the artist's interpretation and, of course, knowledge of the subject.

Without such knowledge, interpretation for the purpose of carving is impossible. Notice in Figure 8–9 that the gouge marks (at the center chalkline) move to the left and to the right, away from the line. This movement pushes the wood back at the line, thus raising a profile. Gouge strokes at the top move upward—the best stroke with which to cope with tough top end grain.

Motion is the theme of the sculpture. The modeling of details is postponed until the major design is worked out.

As *Torso in Motion* progressed, I decided to intensify its twisting motion. The chalkline marking the high point at the center was swung harder off center as it snaked downward (see Figure 8–10). The slanted line that indicated a raised hip at the beginning of the sculpture has now become a reality and does not need the chalkline. The raised hip conforms to the movements of a torso with the weight placed on one leg as the other leg strides. By glancing at the base and observing the uncarved portions of the wood, and then by looking at the upper carved portions, it can be seen that the original circular log is being converted into angular planes. The wood was the same diameter from top to bottom, but the varied planes created by carving cause the carved portions of the wood to assume larger visual proportions than those of the original confines of the log (see Figure 8–10).

The carving activity has now moved down to encompass almost the entire length of the log. The legs of the torso are sought for, in the lowest section of the carving. Since this is to be a torso,

FIGURE 8–10 The wood was the same diameter from top to bottom before carving, but the varied planes created by the carving caused the carved portions to assume larger visual proportions than those of the original confines. (Photo by Chee Heng Yeong)

which is a fraction of the whole human figure, for the sake of unity of design, I plan to carve not the whole legs but a fraction of both, stopping above the knee. Look at Figure 8–10 and notice that although two legs are to be carved in order to support the torso, the whole mass of wood in the lower area of the sculpture is being treated as one form. This treatment of two or more forms as one mass during the early stages of a carving is crucial to the success of a sculpture that is carved directly. I can safely say that the early separation between two forms is the beginner's most frequent mistake and the most prevalent cause of first-attempt failure. The chisels and gouges must be able to roam freely from one form to the next. If there is a separation, the tools will move into the separation in order to complete the cut. If the cut is stopped short of the separation, then a new depression will begin to emerge. Eventually, all attempts to develop the two forms touching each other would only serve to widen the gap. With this in mind, use

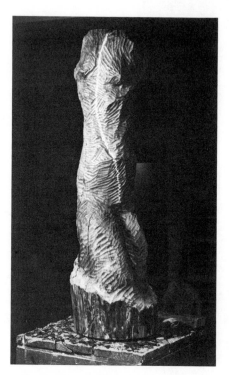

FIGURE 8–11 *Torso in Motion* completed. The separation dividing one leg from the other was made after both legs related properly to their function in this design. One leg is flexed in motion; the other bears the full weight of the torso. (Photo by Gil McMillon)

chalklines to define separations between units and keep the gaps between them undefined for as long as the sculpture continues to change and develop.

The time to separate the legs in the sculpture of *Torso in Motion* would be after I have related the masses of one leg to the next. In order to do this, I must ask questions: Which leg is advanced? Which one is further back than the other? How do the legs relate to the torso they support? They must be pushed back into the wood mass deeply enough to seem to belong to the torso. To bring about these desirable design relationships, more and more wood must be carved off. And to do this, the mass of wood that is to accommodate both legs must be united as a single large plane (see Figure 8–11).

9

laminated wood

LAMINATED wood means the joining of pieces of wood with glue or other adherents so that the joined pieces form a whole. The pieces to be laminated can be as thick as boards or planks, or they can be as thin as veneer. Though furniture designers laminate paper-thin veneer, the woodcarver limits the thinness of veneer laminants to ⅛ inch. If veneers thinner than ⅛ inch are laminated for carving, not enough carvable wood will be present between glue joints. Boards and planks of any thickness can be laminated into a solid carvable block. The span of the clamps is the only limitation to the girth of the lamination.

The sculpture in Figure 9–1 by Carl Talley was carved from laminated pine planks. The legs and tail were laminated and carved separately and then attached to the body with ½-inch dowels. Glue was introduced into the holes drilled in order to accommodate the dowels. Lamination expands the direct-carving concept. If Carl Talley intended to have his sculpture of a greyhound running, and if he further intended to carve a group of greyhounds running instead of just one, only by using the laminated wood technique could such a sculpture be feasible in direct woodcarving, considering that the scale of the greyhound sculpture is life size. Certainly, by laminating legs, body, and tail separately, the sculptor made good use of the possibilities of lamination. The visibility of some of the seams between planks does not detract from the piece; instead, it adds to it. The integrity of the method or technique used is as much a part of the sculpture as the context and design.

how to laminate　The prerequisites to successful lamination are that the surfaces of the wood to be laminated must be smooth and flat. A reliable glue must be applied to the surfaces to be joined, and clamps are then applied for needed pressure. If boards or planks to be laminated are obtained rough surfaced, they

FIGURE 9–1 *Greyhound* by Carl Talley. The legs and tail were laminated and carved separately, then doweled to the body. (Photo by Gil McMillon)

must be planed and joined, terms used to describe the machine process which smoothes both sides of the boards so that they fit snugly together. The woodcarver need not own machinery for planing and joining wood. Many lumber yards offer the service. It is called "milling" in lumber-yard jargon. Individual cabinetmakers and industrial wood-workers also offer milling service. The wood to be laminated may be obtained premilled from most lumber dealers. The advantages of obtaining un-milled wood for lamination are that it frees the sculptor to find odd shapes and unusual woods; also, rough woods are much cheaper than pre-milled woods. Wood glues are plentiful. Hardware stores will have many brands and types. Some are organic, and some are plastic resins. All are reliable and tough, especially those manufactured by chemical companies with famous names.

Some glues are sold ready-mixed, but the nature of others prevents this. The plastic resin glues are sold in powdered form with clear directions for mixing. All plastic resin glues have a limited shelf life—the maximum time it can be stored before becoming useless. It would not help to list the shelf lives of resin glues here because these vary with the brands and changes as manufacturers try to improve their products. If it is not written on the label, ask the hardware dealer about the shelf life of the glue. Titebond glue is one of my favorite glues because it is obtainable ready-mixed, it can sit on the shelf for months and still work, and it is also tough. Cascemite and Weldwood glues are plastic resin glues obtainable in a powdered state. Portions of the powder are mixed with water as needed. Cascemite and Weldwood glues are tenacious binders and are preferred by furniture designers. Both glues are excellent for woodcarvers working with laminated wood. Read the mixing directions on the label. Observe the clamping and drying times suggested by the manufacturer.

I have adopted a method of supporting the glue when laminating heavy planks. I use wooden dowels or pegs to pin the planks in spite of the glue, just to make sure. The dowels are driven into drilled holes the next day—after the glue is dry. For small work, ⅜-inch diameter dowels are adequate. Use ¾- or 1-inch dowels for larger works. The dowels appear in the carving, but they can be blended with the general color of the sculpture by tinting them with an appropriate stain. Some sculptors apply glue to both facing surfaces to be glued. I prefer a lean glue application; therefore, I always apply glue only to one side of the two surfaces to be glued. When only one side is smeared with glue, there is less sliding when clamps are applied. But more important, the glue joints are thinner and less visible. Too much glue builds up a glue body between boards. The end grain of the wood will not join. All lamination must be long grain against long grain. If, after gluing and clamping, the work should fail to adhere, replane the surfaces and check your glue supply; it may be old stock, or if ready mixed, your dealer may be making mixing errors.

After applying the glue, the next stage in laminating is to clamp. Much pressure is required to assist the glue to bind the wood into a single unit. If the breadth of the project requires a large number of pieces of wood, then it is better to glue and clamp small sections at a time. Then, when all of the sections are glued, clamped, and dry, join them all into one unit. The reason for this is that the glues are quick-setting. Some set in 20 minutes, others in 10 to 15 minutes. It would never do to glue so many pieces that when piece number 20 is being glued, the glue is set hard and dry on pieces 1, 2, and 3. For example, if the total width of the project requires 24 boards 1 inch thick, divide them into three batches of eight boards each; then, when all batches are dry, unite them. If possible, work with a helper.

The type of clamps used depends on the width of the work (see Figure 9–2 for examples). For small work, "C" clamps will do. If the work is larger than a foot in width, bar clamps are best. For very wide laminations, use pipe clamps. Pipe clamps are expandable; by the simple expediency of removing the clamps and obtaining a longer pipe, one can extend the pipe clamp. For very thin veneers, use a clamp every 4 inches. For large work consisting of boards or planks, use a clamp every 12 inches. Clamping cannot be overdone. Respond to your visual observation of what is happening and apply clamps where they are needed.

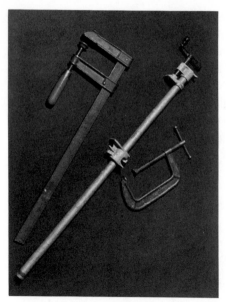

FIGURE 9–2 Three basic clamps
suitable for clamping glued boards. Top:
Bar clamp 2 feet long; center: pipe clamp
3 feet long; bottom: a 6-inch clamp for
small-scale work. (Photo by Chee Heng
Yeong)

**journal of
a sculpture in
laminated red oak**

Sculptor Norma Anderson executed a sculpture commission in laminated red oak. The sculpture was commissioned as a memorial, and its subject was to be *The Holy Family*. It measures 6 feet high, 3 feet wide, and is 10 inches in depth. The planks were obtained in the rough—unmilled. When the planks were obtained, they had been air-dried out of doors for eight months. They were brought indoors, carefully stacked, and allowed to dry for 6 months.

After they were planed and joined, the sculptor decided that eighteen heavy planks, most over 6 feet long, were too many to glue and clamp in a single batch, since the Titebond glue used for this project dries in 20 minutes. The sculptor decided to divide the planks into three batches. The seven planks of the first batch were stood on end against a wall (see Figure 9–3). While the planks were in this position, glue was applied with 2-inch paint brushes.

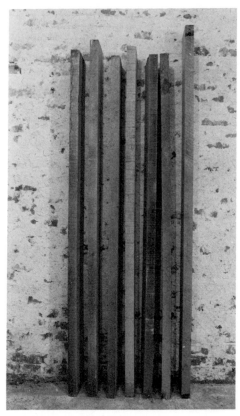

FIGURE 9–3 The seven planks of the first batch were stood on end against a wall. While in this position, the glue was applied with a paintbrush. (Photo by Gordon Cruz

Because the gluing process demands speed, Norma Anderson used a helper. Glue was applied to both sides of the surfaces to be attached. Clamps were immediately applied after the surfaces of the boards were painted with the glue. Notice that the pipe clamps used in Figure 9–4 were placed in opposing pairs. Two clamps were placed every 12 inches, and finally, two were added at both ends. The pressure applied by the clamps makes the crucial difference. When clamping, tighten the clamps to the utmost. Although Titebond glue dries in 20 minutes, the cautious sculptor waited one day before removing the clamps. Experience teaches that there are exceptions to rules, and certain weather or other condi-

FIGURE 9–4 Pipe clamps are used to clamp the 14-inch width of the boards together. Notice that the 2-inch thickness of the boards as stacked produces the 3-foot width of the sculpture. (Photo by Gordon Cruz)

tions can retard the drying time of the glue. The process described above was repeated with two other sections of oak planks. Before the three sections of planks were joined, three ¾-inch wood dowels were driven crosswise into each section. A 12-inch-long, ¾-inch marine wood bit was used to prepare the holes for the dowels. Notice in Figure 9–4 that the planks are stacked in such a way that their 2-inch thickness will add up to become the 3-foot width of the sculpture. This method provides a greater long-grain surface for gluing and contributes to a stronger glue bond.

Commissions are not done in the same freewheeling spirit that a sculptor uses to produce works of his or her own choice. But a commission can be good for that same reason. It introduces an element of discipline—a bad word for an artist—and it stops one from talking to oneself. In this instance, sculptor Norma Anderson had considerable freedom. A photograph of the clay model (Figure 9–5) was sent to the person commissioning the sculpture. Once approval of the design was obtained, the impermanent clay model was transferred to a plaster of Paris cast—a process that is not described here.

Because the laminated wood mass is 6 feet high, 3 feet broad, and only 10 inches thick, this demands

FIGURE 9–5 With few exceptions, when a sculptor is commissioned to execute a work, a clear model is required. Sculptor Norma Anderson used clay to make a half-scale model of her sculpture of *The Holy Family*. (Photo by the artist)

a high relief style—that is, the figures cannot be carved completely in the round. This choice was made because the sculpture was to be hung on a wall above eye level. The sculpture cannot be called a true relief because some of the figures appear to be almost in the round. The technique used exploits both relief and in-the-round styles. Since the wood will not imitate the clay exactly, the sculptor is free to do a new sculpture from the model. Sculpture done in relief must be carved in the same position in which it is to be viewed.

With the plaster cast model hung a few feet away, Norma Anderson confronted the large mass of laminated oak planks. It is never easy, but always exciting—that first confrontation the sculptor has with a blank mass of materials to which he or she must give life. In this case, because of the model, the sculptor had worked out all of the highest points of the sculpture. When the human figure is standing in repose, the head is usually the highest projection forward; when seated, the high point shifts to the limbs. In the proposed sculpture of *The Holy Family,* the sculptor's design involves one seated and two standing figures. The knee of the seated figure of the mother is the highest point of the entire sculpture. Next is the head of the mother and then the head of the child; the standing figure of Joseph is found furthest into the depth of the wood. The artist made a very rough drawing with charcoal, which was only intended to start things, not to fix them, because with the first strokes of the chisels, the surface of the wood changes, resulting in a bypass of the lines previously drawn. Drawings on the surface of the sculpture involve a constant reassessment and adjustment of high points and low points.

Figures 9–6 and 9–7 show the heads of the three figures emerging from the wood as if by magic. The head at the top reveals the correct method of carving from the high point to the low, making no firm commitment toward clarity in the early stages.

FIGURE 9–6 The heads of the three figures are emerging as if by magic. An important rule is that the wood sculpture must be carved in the position in which it is to be mounted for viewing. (Photo by the artist)

FIGURE 9–7 A very tentative step forward. The head of the child and that of Joseph are slightly and cautiously clearer. (Photo by the artist)

The technique of moving from a tentative rough-out to clearly defined carving is shown in Figures 9–8 and 9–9. All forms that are to touch each other, such as the two heads, should remain touching as the sculpture develops. Notice that no attempt has been made to separate the figure of the child from that of the mother. Neither has any thought been given to the arms and hands of the mother and child. Compare this stage with the clay model in Figure 9–5 and see the complex forms that need to be carved between the child's arms and hands and those of the mother. The vigor of the gouge marks reflects the sculptor's excitement and her re-action to the forms revealed by the carving process (see Figure 9–10). The wood is no longer a static, shapeless mass. It is energy and movement, and it lives. The tool marks describe both the forms and their texture. Upstrokes, cross-strokes, and down-strokes intermingle and vibrate. The tools used to

FIGURE 9–8 The technique of moving from tentative rough-out to clear carving. (Photo by the artist)

FIGURE 9–9 The heads of the two figures and the drapery above them have become much clearer. The mother's fond touching of her cheek against the child's cheek has been maintained. Inexperienced carvers sometimes cause touching forms to separate by working too deeply into the spaces between the touching forms. (Photo by the artist)

remove excess wood become a means of expressing the artist's mood. The hands of the mother and child in Figure 9–10 are being tentatively sought with probes of the small gouges. The seams between the laminated planks are invisible in the smoothed face of the mother. The seams always become less visible as the carving moves down below the original surface. The highest points on the heads of the mother and child are noses, then foreheads, and then chins; in that order, the sculptor probed in search of these shapes. As we saw in Figure 9–6, the sculptor clarified the heads of the figures before seeking the shapes that were most recessed. Never try to find the lowest points first; move in from the higher planes.

The plaster model was discarded at this stage, the sculptor preferring to work from photographs of the model instead. It was a wise decision, because the wood began to respond to the gouges by yielding its own undulating forms as well as its own energy. In general, the design remained faithful to the original model, but in vital detail the character of the wood imposed itself. In this full-length view of the laminated wood sculpture of *The Holy Family*, Norma Anderson has all the figures clearly placed. Arms and hands are sketched in. Feet are not yet sought. The differences in tone that can be seen in the wood surfaces (see Figure 9–11) are caused by the sculptor's habit of applying Danish oil to the work during the carving process, hoping to retard the rapidly drying wood after it had been placed in

FIGURE 9–10 The vigor of the gouge marks reflects the sculptor's excitement. (Photo by the artist)

FIGURE 9–11 In this full-length view of *The Holy Family*, Norma Anderson has all of the figures clearly placed. (Photo by Gordon Cruz)

the warm studio. The oil darkens the wood; the light tones visible are the freshly carved areas. Notice how important the high points are to the sculpture. Knowing where the high points are is knowing the place from which to carve inward into the wood. The knee of the seated figure of the mother is the highest point of this sculpture. It thrusts farther into space than the rest of the sculpture. All else is recessed. The standing figure in the background is the most recessed. Because the laminated wood is only 10 inches thick, the sculptor had to work out the various projections and depressions within the total 10-inch thickness available.

The sculpture of *The Holy Family* in laminated red oak is shown completed in Figure 9–12. The sculpture has been oiled in preparation for filling its

FIGURE 9–12 The finished sculpture of *The Holy Family* by Norma Anderson (Commissioned by Barbara A. [Fisher] Busch in memory of Harold Fisher. Courtesy of Trinity Episcopal Church, Fort Wayne, Indiana; photo by Chee Heng Yeong)

small crevices with wax. If the reader turns to Figure 9–4 and then to Figure 9–6, he or she can see the sculpture move from mere planks in the former to a vibrant presence in the latter stage. Undeniably, the process or journey in the carving of a sculpture is the most stimulating part to the sculptor. His or her immediate reactions to what happens when some wood chips fly off, leaving a specific shape, influences what happens next.

The finished piece is, of course, the triumph of the whole effort: It pleases the sculptor and excites others.

The standing father figure of Joseph in the background was left textured with chisel and gouge marks. One should not remove all texture and then put chisel marks where required. Chisel marks created in such an artificial manner look self-conscious and contrived. The tool marks in the finished sculpture shown here are a "living" texture that occurred as the sculpture developed. When it is desirable to finish a piece with a combined smooth and rough surface, remove texture slowly, always observing the effect; if not sure, give the existing texture the benefit of the doubt. I once carved a 7-foot-high figure of a man. When I removed all of the texture, the surface looked like skin instead of wood. My aim was to do a sculpture in wood; therefore, an imitation of nature was uncomfortable and spoiled the sculpture. I had to recarve the entire piece in order to regain an honest texture. If texture is removed and then is needed, try to renew it by recarving the area to be retextured instead of just putting in texture.

This chapter on laminated wood does not attempt to deal with all of the possibilities obtainable in the wood lamination technique. The reason is that some aspects of wood lamination are more applicable to forms of sculpture not related to direct carving. Also, many of the laminated-wood techniques are most applicable to furniture design. Since our discussion here is focused on wood lamination for direct carving, I dealt mainly with the construction of a carvable block or mass of wood that had been prepared for the purpose of carving. The technique enables the sculptor to work with dimensions and shapes unobtainable in logs of wood. Different colors and types of wood can be blended or contrasted in a single work. Care should be taken when mixing different colors of wood to avoid jarring contrasts, unless these will enhance the sculpture.

10

**finishing
wood
sculpture**

SCULPTURE in wood lasts longer—far longer—when kept indoors. Despite weather-proofing, and even with the abundance of available weather-proofing substances for wood, a sculpture in wood, placed out of doors, will still deteriorate sooner than a similar sculpture kept indoors. This does not mean that wood sculpture should not be placed out of doors and exposed to weather. But when this is done, it should be done with the anticipation that the piece will eventually suffer weather damage.

Finishing sculpture in wood involves sanding, scraping, and the application of oils, stains, dyes, and sometimes paints and lacquers to the finished work. The beauty of wood intensifies when treated and pampered with polishing oils. Polishing a piece of sculpture in wood does not necessarily mean smoothing it or ridding it of all texture. A sculpture in wood can be finished without removing the tool marks, or it can be smoothed free of all tool marks before finishing. The finished sculpture can also have a combination of chisel texture and smooth surface.

The ritual of sanding, scraping, and finishing or polishing wood sculpture is as full of personal anecdote as homespun remedies for coughs and colds. Every sculptor has a secret formula. Many good wood-finishing oils, stains, and varnishes are available at hardware stores. Most are excellent. One's own taste is usually the decisive factor as to which finishing agent is used. Most sculptors prefer to use finishes that leave the wood in its natural state. To such sculptors, staining is a last resort that is only used if the wood has discolorations or if there are strong contrasting knots or grains in the wrong places on the sculpture. However, many sculptors plan to stain their work as a way of finishing the sculpture. The stains are used to introduce color harmonies to the piece. Sometimes staining is used because knots and other blemishes appear discordantly, especially in light-colored woods, such as maple or ash. My own preference is to leave the wood sculpture as natural as possible, using stains only when absolutely necessary to blend discordant blotches. A wood sculpture that includes sapwood and heartwood may have contrasting colors that may affect the sculpture adversely; then, certainly, staining is advisable.

applying an oil finish

The most common wood finish used by sculptors is a combination of boiled linseed oil and turpentine, mixed in equal parts. This mixture can be used on any kind of wood with no bad effects. Light-colored wood, such as maple and ash, will be slightly yellowed by the oil-turpentine mix, but not in a harmful way. The mixture causes a golden yellow and accents the veining or grains of the wood. Many sculptors try very hard to find a wood-finishing oil that leaves the sculpture totally natural. Such an oil is very hard to find, but it seems that if a polishing agent leaves no sign of its presence after it is used, there is hardly any need to apply it, except for protective reasons. Before applying linseed oil–turpentine mix to the finished wood sculpture, make sure that dust or wood shavings are removed. I use a vacuum cleaner for dust and shavings removal or simply dust the sculpture with a dry brush.

Mix equal parts of linseed oil and turpentine in a glass jar with a wide top. The first and second coats can be applied within two hours of each other. A housepainter's brush is good enough to apply the mix. Wait a day or two before applying one or more additional coats, as desired. The eye is the judge as to how many coats are needed.

Very often, after a sculpture is oiled, forms that seemed finished suddenly appear to need more work. Should further carving or sanding be necessary after the work has been oiled, let the oil and turpentine dry before attempting to sand. But carving can be done while the oil is still wet. If there are any checks in the wood, fill them with softened petroleum or beeswax immediately after the first coat of oil is applied. When the oil–turpentine application is thoroughly dried, the whole surface can be further enriched by an application of Butcher's wax. A week or more should pass before the wax is applied. Butcher's wax is a hard, transparent wax intended for polishing wood furniture. It is available at hardware stores. To apply Butcher's wax, use a polishing cloth that will not shred or shed threads or lint. Rub small portions of wax evenly over the surface of the sculpture. Rub in. After all of the sculpture has been waxed, buff it vigorously with a dry cloth. The buffed sculpture obtains a pleasing, dull sheen.

Another popular and excellent finisher is Danish oil. It is especially preferred for use on light-colored wood, because it has a less yellowing effect than linseed oil. Danish oil penetrates into the wood. Usually, two coats are enough. Danish oil begins to gloss if more than two coats are applied. The surface of the sculpture can be worked after Danish oil is applied. It is a very good habit to try out oils and stains on a piece of scrapboard and then to observe the results before tackling the actual sculpture.

removing texture Whenever a totally smooth surface is desirable in order to show off the sculptured forms to the fullest advantage, all texture should be removed and the surface should be sanded before any polishing oils are applied. Removing the texture left by the gouges must be done carefully. The sculptor cannot just simply remove texture, because the forms may deteriorate if the texture removal is not treated as an essential part of the carving. Chisels, rather than rasps or files, should be the first tools to use in texture removal. The gouges used to carve the wood leave grooves on its surface. Some of these grooves can be as deep as 1 inch. If one were to rasp or file down to such a depth, control of the sculptured shapes would be lost. On the other hand, the use of a chisel to carve down texture enables the sculptor to remove the gouge marks while maintaining or even improving the carved shapes. Use a firmer chisel, beveled on both sides, to start the texture removal. A short-bend flat chisel is a very good chisel to use for finishing, especially if the wood is very loose-grained and tends to shred when chiseled. After the wood is chiseled to a nearly smooth surface in areas where smoothness is desired, then it is time to apply rasps and files.

A good wood rasp for general use is a sureform rasp, obtainable in hardware stores (see Figure 10–1). The semicircular blade is much better for the sculptor's use than a flat blade. Usually, the dealer has both types of blades. Ask for the semicircular one. Rifflers are excellent for filing small works or for use on details. Shadows on wood sculpture are darker in tone if the surface of the wood is rough. Because of this, after texture is removed, it may be necessary to recarve or deepen the undercuts. Use chisels, not gouges, to deepen undercuts on a finished piece. Rasping and filing need not be a separate operation from chiseling; sometimes all of

FIGURE 10–1 Two views of a sureform wood rasp. (Photo by Gordon Cruz)

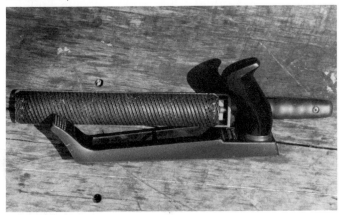

these can be done in support of each other during the finishing process.

sanding When the surface of the wood sculpture is sufficiently free of gouge marks, sanding and scraping are the next steps to be taken towards finishing. A flat chisel is a good scraper. Hold the chisel with both hands—one hand on the handle, the other on the upper part of the blade. Place the chisel in an upright position at right angles to the wood surface and push and pull to scrape. Hardware stores and woodwork dealers sell various tools designed for scraping wood.

Sanding the sculpture brings it to the completely finished stage, leaving only oiling, waxing, or staining as the last of the finishing rituals. Observe existing shapes before sanding, and try to maintain them during the sanding.

Too much pressure on the sandpaper causes lumps on the surface of the wood. It helps to wrap the sandpaper around a small block of wood; then, hold the wood in the palm of the hand and sand the sculpture by moving the wood block back and forth. The wood block helps to save fingers from being sanded at the same time that it enables a more even sanding than when the sandpaper is simply pressed against the wood with the fingers.

Another good sandpaper holder, especially for sanding hollows and details, is a wooden dowel. Wrap the sandpaper tightly around a dowel, the size of which will be determined by the scale of the area to be sanded. Use one end of the dowel as a handle and rotate or push and pull the sandpaper-wrapped end along the area to be sanded.

Sandpaper for wood is a most flourishing and available product that is sold at hardware stores. There are so many good brands that no attempt will be made here to recommend any particular type, other than to list my own preferences. I have noticed that sanding by hand should start with a coarse paper. This is important. If sanding starts with a medium or fine grain paper, nothing will be accomplished. The wood will retain its unevenness. From coarse, move to medium and then to fine and extra fine. I favor aluminum oxide sandpaper, although many other types of sandpaper are just as effective.

staining

Staining the finished sculpture is a prevailing practice of many woodcarving sculptors. It is often difficult to decide whether to leave the wood natural or whether to stain it. Staining is sometimes used when the surface of the finished wood sculpture has knots appearing in places where they mar the forms, or when a great deal of contrasting sapwood is included in the carving. Sometimes, staining is used if the wood is too neutral or uninteresting in color.

Staining need not be used purely to produce consistency in the tones of the finished work. Many sculptors anticipate and include staining as an important part of the finishing. To such sculptors, staining adds color, which becomes an integral part of the sculpture. There are some common woods used by sculptors, such as maple, oak, and mahogany, for which there are namesake stains. Stains bearing the same names as a type of wood closely resemble the tones of the wood they imitate. Such stains are helpful to the sculptor who needs a stain to blend and unify the surface tones of a finished piece of sculpture. But for those who use stains as a means of introducing various colors to the sculpture, stains need not blend with the general tones of the wood. I once stained a sculpture in hickory wood because a knot occurred in the center of the mouth of my carved sculpture of a head. To complicate the tones even more, the deeply colored heartwood was exposed in two places, causing sharply contrasting tones; as a result, the carved head lacked unity of tone, and the overall design fell apart as a result. Staining was the only answer. I decided to mix my own stain.

I used boiled linseed oil and turpentine (equal parts) as a medium into which I squeezed some artist's oil colors. In order to blend the lighter-colored wood with the dark heartwood and knot, the stain had to be as dark as the darkest parts of the wood. With this in mind, I chose burnt sienna and burnt umber as the colors for making the stain. There are no rules for mixing your own stain. Your judgments are the guide. I squeezed some burnt sienna into the oil–turpentine mix, which was contained in a glass jar, stirred, dipped a paint brush in, and tried it on a board. Too reddish. By adding burnt umber slowly, I obtained the desired tone.

Keep the stain mix thin; it is not a paint. More than one coat may be needed. I usually stain the lightest parts of the sculpture first, let them dry, and then stain the whole work.

Oil-based and water-based wood stains are available at any hardware or housepaint supply store. The brands are numerous. I prefer the oil-based stains, but many sculptors choose water-based stains—it's a question of personal choice.

Dyes made for tinting fabrics can be used to stain wood. A wide range of experimentation is possible in using stains. Various colors can be introduced for effect. If the aim in staining is to achieve harmony, try to obtain a stain bearing the same name as the wood, for example, use an oak stain for oak wood. You may ask, "What is the reason for staining a wood sculpture in oak with an oak stain? Is not the natural wood more beautiful than the stain?" Some of the reasons that may invite staining the natural surface are contrasting sapwood, which may have been left on some of the higher planes, causing discordant tones, or knots and contrary grains, which may occur in places where they are not desired. A stain thickly brushed on in some places and thinly washed on in other areas can unify all while still allowing the wood to show through. Some stains are opaque, covering the wood almost as paint does. The thin, transparent stains are best for the sculptor, since they allow more freedom of choice during the application.

Lacquers and shellacs can also be used as wood finishers. However, these are high-gloss by nature and should only be used if a glossy finish is desirable.

painting

From antiquity to present times, woodcarvers have used paints to adorn their sculptures. There are no rules to painting wood carvings. The individual artist's own taste decides, and that is the charm of painted wood sculptures. It is a good idea, but not a necessity, to size the sculpture before painting. The sizing seals the wood and allows you to use only one direct coat of paint. Without a sizer, it may be necessary to paint the same work as many as three times in order to obtain radiant tones.

Rabbit skin glue is an excellent sizer for the woodcarver. Directions for its preparation and use are written on the label of the container in which it is obtained. Artists' supply stores usually stock this glue. One coat is enough, and it has the advantage of being a transparent glue that does not make its presence visible after it is applied to the wood. If rabbit skin glue is unavailable, then any wood-sizing solution obtainable from housepaint supply stores can be used. Today's sculptor has a bigger range of paints to choose from than the sculptors of antiquity. Water-based or oil-based paints, glossy or flat: All of these can be used.

When painting a wood sculpture, try to avoid changing the sculpture into a "painting." Paint the sculpture in such a way as to maintain the integrity of the carved forms. To state this more clearly, let the ins and outs of the carved forms describe the sculpture instead of trying to create the volumes of the work with the paints.

Enamel paints are very good for use in painting wood sculpture, especially if the wood is presized or primed with rabbit skin glue. The enamels are brilliant in appearance, and the surface dries hard and washable.

Flat-drying paints are not as dirt-resistant as enamels. If flat paints are used, then varnish or wax the whole surface later in order to protect the colors from soil. A painter-turned-sculptor will be able to paint the sculpture with ease but must try hard not to change it into a painting. If you are a sculptor who has never painted, you actually have the advantage in painting the finished wood sculpture.

weather-proofing   Although wood sculpture will last longer if it is kept indoors, there are ways of weather-proofing wood sculptures so that they can withstand decay—for a reasonable length of time—when they are placed out of doors. Of course, even when weather-proofed, a wood sculpture placed out of doors for a lengthy period of time will have a limit to its duration.

Some sculptures in wood, such as weathervanes, figureheads for ships' bows, or even wooden carved decorations for buildings, are all designed for outdoors and should be weather-proofed. Painting is the simplest way, but very often, the artist wishes to leave the wood in its natural state.

There are other weather-proofing agents, such as Coprenol and Polyurethane. Both are obtainable at hardware stores, and both are colorless. The labels that accompany them give ample directions for their proper use. Boiled linseed oil and turpentine can be applied after the sculpture is treated with

Coprenol, but not after Polyurethane is used. Polyurethane is an absolute sealer, so that oiling is useless.

making a base

Wood sculptures that are to stand on the ground outside should be elevated slightly off the ground in order to allow for air circulation. The base of a sculpture is most frequently a concern of the finishing and presentation process. A base to a sculpture is as a frame to a painting—it can cause a lot of controversy. After all, since the sculpture is finished, it certainly is not depending on the base for its beauty; mostly, the base serves to prevent the sculpture from falling over. Keep the base in context. Large sculptures that balance by themselves need not have a base. Be sure to apply petroleum or beeswax to the bottom end grain if this area remains after the piece is finished. If the work is completely spherical, then the end grain need not be waxed. After one coat of oil, press wax into all visible cracks at the bottom before attaching the sculpture to the base. Sculptures that are unstable should be attached to a base of wood or any other choice of material. If the base is of wood, simply drill a hole through the wood base into the bottom of the sculpture and tap in a wooden dowel. With one dowel holding the base in place, add one or more other dowels. Use glue on the dowel if the base is to be permanent. Should stone be used as a base, metal pins and epoxy glue should be used instead of wood.

11

carving
and adding

DIRECT carvers, especially those carving in wood, soon arrive at the conclusion that the sculpture can be greatly extended by adding other units to the main structure. The additions may be of the same materials, or they may be of completely different substances.

Carving and adding can be done in both stone and wood, but wood lends itself best to the innovations of added parts. Wood can be more easily glued and joined together than stone, and it is also less weighty. These are the factors that encourage sculptors to experiment most with innovations with wood.

technical
considerations

Carving and adding deals with structure and joints in quite a different way than furniture design or carpentry. If strict joints or academic wood-joining systems are used, such joints or systems will influence the work into conforming to rigid preplanned shapes and will take attention away from the creative considerations in favor of solutions to technical problems.

The sculptor experimenting with carving and adding must make up the joints as needed and create joint systems to suit the aesthetic considerations. Actually, such innovative joints can be a creative detail of the sculpture.

It is helpful if the sculptor doing carving and adding in wood has some experience with carpentry and if the sculptor working in stone knows some elementary masonry. In the absence of such experience, common sense is the next best guide, and adventure provides the incentive.

A sense of adventure in solving the problems of joints can lead to interesting solutions that can greatly enhance the sculpture. Whenever glue is to be used as a bond at joints, not only are a close fit and tight clamping necessary but matching long grain to long grain is essential; end grain does not glue.

The practice of carving and adding other elements to the main sculpture is not an innovation. The method has been used extensively in the past. Ancient sculptors—African, Greek, Egyptian, and Roman—were accustomed to adding other materials to their carvings in wood and stone. Some of the added materials were gold, precious stones, paints, weavings, and fabric.

A large part of ancient sculpture was religious in context, and many of these sculptures were of the crucifix. Sculptors working with this theme often resorted to carving and adding in order to exploit fully the design possibilities offered by the subject.

Sculptures composed of many parts work best if there is a major element, with smaller additions, instead of a series of small parts making up the whole. One major element gives the sculpture its basic structure; then, by adding other sections, the main theme becomes extended.

It is best to carve all units of the sculpture as close as possible to the finish before joining, because the shock of hammer blows during carving can break the joints.

Some joints, such as long grain against long grain, bonded by a good glue, can withstand carving. But joints that are doweled or bolted should not be submitted to the shock of carving. Units that are carved separately but are to be joined together later can be constantly tried out in their proposed positions as the work develops.

Sculptures of animals lend themselves well to the technique of carving and adding. For example, if a sculpture of an animal form requires outspread wings, an extended tail, or even four legs, and if such extensions are to be subtracted from a single block of material, much labor will be involved, as well as an immense waste of materials, if all of these extensions and projections must be extracted from a single block. A direct and creative way to deal with such projecting parts as wings or legs is to carve them separately and then attach them to the main sculpture.

The angle at which added elements will relate to the main sculpture cannot always be predicted and to do so can stifle the creativity of the sculpture. Predictable sculpture is uninteresting sculpture. At the same time, although freedom is a necessary part of creativity, order and strength are important. The joints must hold together. Ninety degree (right angle) joints can be solved by any number of simple and time-proven wood-joining methods. A good right-angle joint is a mortise and tenon joint—literally, a socket and a plug. A socket is cut into the main body of the work, for which an exact fit plug is carved at the end of the element to be joined.

A simple copy of the mortise and tenon is to drill a hole in the body of the work at the spot where the junction of an element is needed; then drill a corresponding hole at the end of the element to be joined. Insert a dowel at the end of the element and drive the doweled end into the prepared hole. Care must be taken to line up the predrilled holes so that the attached part is at the desired angle. The best way to do this is to fasten both elements firmly (use nails or glue) and drill through both while they are in place. This means that the dowel end will show, but this ensures a good fit. The end of the dowel—or any hole left by the dowel—can be smeared with a mix of wood dust and glue.

The dowel used should be the same diameter as the hole, and the size of the dowel is determined by the weight to be supported. The length of the dowel should be slightly less than the combined depth of both the hole in the element and that in the body of the work in order to enable the joined parts to touch.

In the mortise and tenon joint, or its dowel imitation, glue can be used if the joint is not to be removable. In case the joint is to be removable, then the plug should be slightly less than the socket, or the dowel less in diameter than the drilled hole, in order to ensure easy removal. Much can be learned about successful joining by persistence and trial by error. A successful and original solution to a problem can be a great thrill to the artist.

aesthetic considerations

Aesthetic considerations play an important part in carving directly and adding either carved or completely different elements. Use good judgment. One pitfall is the temptation to be too literal with the added portions. If a sculpture of a head in wood or stone has real hair added, the result can be confusing or even repulsive to the senses. However, the same sculpture of a head in wood or stone can be adorned with real jewels, cloth, beads, or metal, and such additions can be visually pleasing. The reason jewels, cloth, beads, and so on are aesthetically pleasing when added to wood or stone is because they are visually compatible with the wood and stone. However, discordant materials can be used as additions to a sculpture if it suits the aims of the sculptor.

examples of carving and adding
"cruz"

The so-called primitive sculptors, those who carved religious sculpture, were well aware of the emotional effects produced by combining visually discordant materials, especially when some of the elements chosen have certain mental associations. The sculptors of Africa, the Caribbean, and the Pacific islands, are exceptionally deft at this type of combination in their religious sculptures. As a child in the Caribbean, and even as an adult, whenever I viewed a voodoo sculpture with its head of painted wood combined with human hair and teeth, the effect on me was always the same: fear and awe. And that is precisely the emotional response sought by the creators of such sculpture.

Cruz, in black walnut (see Figure 11–1), is an example of carving and adding in wood. Both arms of the figure are extended about 2½ feet from the body. Instead of finding a log wide enough to contain such an extension, it was better to add the arms. Also, such additions created added drama in the subject. The same reasoning encouraged me to construct and add the cross. In my first try at adding the arms, I decided upon a mortise and tenon joint. This soon proved to be a mistake. Marking out a square 2½ inches at the spot where the arms are to adjoin the body, I used a chisel to scoop out a socket 3 inches deep. At the end of the walnut extensions that were selected as arms, I

FIGURE 11–1 *Cruz* by Arnold Prince (black walnut; 10 feet high by 5 feet wide). (Photo by Phillip Knopp)

fashioned a plug that was the same size as the socket. When all was ready, I hammered in the arms with a heavy sledge hammer. Both arms sprouted out of the sculpture like hat racks. Clearly, the joints chosen were the wrong ones. Removing the arms could not be done by pulling them out because the plug and the socket were the same size. I had to saw off both arms.

To attach both arms so that they would appear to spring naturally from the figure, I created a joint that causes the arms to rest upon the body at the shoulders instead of being inserted. The method I used was to cut a notch at the end of the two pieces of wood that were to serve as arms. The notches were half the circumference of the wood. The two areas where the notched ends were to be attached were thoroughly flattened and sanded. When both notches as well as their rests were flat enough to fit, I pinned the arms in place with ½-inch-diameter lag bolts 3 inches long. I used two bolts for each joint.

Next came the forearms. I did not wish to follow the general crucifix posture of outstretched arms. Bending the arms at the elbows with the fingers pointing downwards seemed to add to the drama I sought to depict in this sculpture of the crucifix. After selecting two pieces of walnut to use as forearms, I carved them into the general shape of forearms, working not for an imitation of the forearms but for a design based upon them. When all was ready, I cut notches at the ends of these units. I made the notches with very little effort. By simply sawing a scoreline down to the depth that the notches were to be and then chiseling away the extra wood, chiseling toward the scoreline, the surplus wood was removed. The notched ends were then bolted to the end grain of the two logs forming the upper arms. The character of the added forms complemented the main body of the sculpture. Noticing this, I decided to exploit the idea even more by adding fingers instead of carving them. I wanted the fingers to be in the same spirit as the arms. Strips of 2" x 2" were cut from walnut boards, and after some experimentation, the hands and fingers were created. These were doweled in position without previous planning.

The cross that completes the sculpture, *Cruz,* is made of 2" x 10" fir planks. These are attached with 1-inch-diameter dowels.

All of the attachments described above were done in the same creative way as the carving. Solutions were found to suit the problems presented, and those problems were considered to be creative challenges.

"toucan" *Toucan,* by Betsy Weiss, is an interesting composite sculpture that uses not only a combination of separately carved units but also has bronze added. The feet, one of which can be seen in Figure 11–2, are made of cast bronze. The head and body of the bird sculpture are carved from walnut; the huge beak from mahoghany; and the tail is mahogany, walnut, and intense red African Padank. With all of these richly colored woods contrasted against each other and complemented by bronze, this sculpture is indeed a successful exploitation of the carving and assembling technique. The beak is attached to the head by two dowels, which were inserted by drilling holes through the beak and into the walnut that forms the head. The dowel ends were left visible. The tail piece is also attached by dowels, which are left visible as part of the design.

The bronze legs and feet have built-in spikes (much like the shank of a knife). These spike ends were driven in to attach the legs. An elm log serves as a base.

"migrating geese" One day I went to the local dump in search of interesting wood shapes, and I found a piece of willow that had a sheared-off top, probably caused when the tree fell. The extension at the top looked

FIGURE 11–2 *Toucan* by Betsy Weiss. (Photo by Gil McMillon)

like a wing, and it was to become the extended wing of the upper bird in *Migrating Geese,* shown in Figure 11–3.

I carved the three bird forms from the single willow log in totem-pole fashion, leaving small connecting ties between each bird. The sculpture did not work well enough in totem-pole design. The feeling of flight was absent. I reacted to this by cutting all of the birds apart, using a "bow saw." This allowed me the freedom to rearrange the composition instead of accepting it as it came out of the block. In the new arrangement, the top and bottom figures are connected at the same joint that they were carved with, but I turned the top figure so that it faced in a new direction, which served the composition much better.

The bird off to the right was at the bottom of the

FIGURE 11–3 *Migrating Geese* by Arnold Prince. (Private collection, Cranston, Rhode Island; photo by Gil McMillon)

totem pole in the original carving. It looked oppressed by the weight of the other two and certainly did not give the feeling of flight. After cutting it away from the rest of the sculpture, I bolted a length of 2″ by 4″ fir to the joint. When the 2″ x 4″ was attached to the main sculpture, it gave the whole work a thrust into space. The 2″ x 4″ fir that provided the extension into space became the support on which I designed a wing by adding feather-shaped wood cut out on a band saw.

Early in the conception of the sculpture, *Migrating Geese,* I intended to use additional pieces of wood to create the wing designs. Walnut and a light-colored African mahogany were used for the additions to the wings. The walnut is black, and the mahogany is very light-colored; therefore, the contrasting colors had to be carefully controlled. If the colors had been used at random, the overall shapes of the wings would have been broken up and would have become ineffective.

The electric-powered band saw is the ideal equipment for making cuts from boards in order to provide added parts to a sculpture. The band saw is not a precision instrument; the sculptor using one can experiment with freeform cuts.

For the additions that complement the wing shapes in Figure 11–3, I first penciled a few different designs on the board and then cut them out on the band saw, making as many as three dozen pieces. These I clamped in place with small "C" clamps for a trial view. Sometimes a week of trial and experiment would take place before I made the final commitment to any specific design. Once a design was adopted, the tips of the wood to be attached were dipped or smeared with a wood glue, clamped in place, allowed to dry, and then doweled. No attempt has been made to hide the presence of the dowels; they are an integral part of the design.

When the sculpture was completed, the willow wood (from which the main body of the work was carved) was treated with a thin oil stain made from equal parts of linseed oil and turpentine into which red and green oil paints were introduced in order to produce very desirable tones on the wood. After the stain dried, the whole sculpture was given three coats of the linseed oil/turpentine equal parts mix.

"gymnast"

Gymnast is composed of three removable parts (see Figure 11–4). The figure was carved from a single oak log. The log was placed in a parallel rather than a vertical position, enabling the sculptor Sheila Krouse to extract the extended legs from the log. If the log was turned vertically, then the legs would have had to be added.

The gymnastic horse over which the figure gracefully hurdles is of two units—oak and cherry. The

FIGURE 11–4 *Gymnast* by Sheila Krouse. (Photo by Vince Ferri)

three pieces of wood making up this sculpture were carved separately, fitted together, and held in place with dowels. The joints are very simple. Holes drilled into the ends of the pieces to be joined accommodate dowels. The dowels are slightly smaller in diameter than the holes in order to allow their easy assembling and disassembling. Motion and grace are depicted in this work. The sculpture is finished with all of the chisel marks left on the surface. Two coats of Danish oil gave it its final embellishment.

"porcupine" *Porcupine* is an unusual work that combines black walnut with fishbones. Here, the artist, Catherine Lebel Schaefer, carved a sculpture of a porcupine in walnut in anticipation of adding a design of "quills" to the sculpture by inserting fish bones into predrilled holes. A tough epoxy was used to hold the bones in place.

The fish bones were not chosen at random but were carefully selected for their individual curve and shape. Notice that the contours of the curves of the porcupine's profile have been maintained by the bones as they extend into space (see Figure 11–5). The lighter-colored portions seen on the legs of the porcupine are caused by the inclusion of the sapwood with the darker heartwood. This is a very original piece of work and does demonstrate that, in the free style of carving and adding, the sculptor can broaden the range.

John Bozarth is a sculptor whose works are in diversified materials that are often combined after the units are carved. In Figure 11–6, Bozarth combines wood with alabaster and limestone. A sculpture of an apple in wood is balanced in the mouth of a form carved in alabaster. The alabaster form sits upon the head of a female with long braids, which, in turn, supports the head as it rests upon a limestone base shaped like a vase. A fish in alabaster

"wood and stone"

FIGURE 11–5 *Porcupine* by Catherine Lebel Schaefer. (Photo by Gil McMillon)

FIGURE 11–6 *Wood and Stone* by John Bozarth. (Photo by Gordon Cruz)

FIGURE 11–7 *Leda and the Swan* by John Bozarth. (Photo by Gordon Cruz)

peers cautiously between the braids. All units are held together with metal pins. No glue or epoxy was used, enabling the sculpture to be taken apart for moving.

Leda and the Swan, Figure 11-7, also by John Bozarth, is another example of a graceful composition using carved and added elements to make a sculpture. The piece was carved from elm wood.

"leda and the swan"

12

**relief
sculpture**

CARVING in relief literally means that the sculpture does not describe the forms completely in the round. The sculptor working in relief uses devices very similar to those used in drawing and painting to create visual illusions of perspective, roundness, and overlapping forms.

In relief sculpture, the forms can be quite flat, yet they may seem to be round. Slight elevations of one plane above another can create a shadow that amplifies the extent of the elevation.

The commonest example of the art of relief sculpture can be seen on any coin or medal. Coins and medals are not carved but are modeled in soft materials and then cast in metal. But the techniques used to create the illusions of distance and roundness are similar to those adapted for use in relief sculpture in wood or stone.

Relief carvings in wood or stone are not limited when compared to carving in the round. To the contrary, relief carving has a broader range of subject matter when compared to free-standing carving in the round. Some of the relief sculptures of antiquity contain huge panoramas of battle scenes, including horses, soldiers, buildings, trees, and sky—all on a small, flat panel. When looking at such a sculpture, one is immediately struck with the fact that the subjects depicted are broader in scope than those dealt with in three-dimensional carving; indeed, relief sculpture matches in subject range that of the painter. Relief is the most familiar form of carving because it is used extensively on furniture. It is inscribed as a decorative pattern on pottery and even on the surface of some wooden cooking utensils. The wooden doors of churches are quite frequently decorated with relief carvings. Architecture, particularly old buildings made of stone, is decorated with relief sculpture—sometimes in floral patterns, often in geometric designs.

The illustration in Figure 12–1 shows one of the

FIGURE 12-1 Relief sculpture sign by Ann Jon. The leaf, twig, and berries are raised above the level of the background. So are the letters of the word "Wheatleigh" and the design below it. The rest of the letters are incised (depressed) below the level of the background plane. (Photo by the artist)

many uses to which relief sculpture is applied where it comes into visual contact with people every day—more so than sculpture in the round. The twigs, berries, and leaves are all raised above the level of the background plane. The letters of the word, "Wheatleigh," and the design below the word are also raised, whereas the other letter is incized (depressed). The design was finished with enamel paints and lacquer: It is a handsome work.

Tombstone makers, who use granite most often to make their tombstones, use the relief carving technique for embellishment and lettering. Tombstone sculptors use pneumatic tools to work the granite and sandblasting guns to cut the lettering. As a result, a stroll through a graveyard is a look at a gallery of relief carving in stone.

technique The tools needed for carving relief sculpture in stone are the same as those used for carving stone in the round—a hammer, points, and toothed and flat chisels. If the stone is soft, the chisels can be used much more than the point, because only shallow cuts are needed to define the inscribed shapes of relief carving. But in hard stones, such as marbles, the point must be used to rough out most of the design, whereas the chisels are reserved for the modeling of details. Finishing a relief sculpture in stone requires the same methods that were described in Chapter 5 on the finishing and polishing of stones.

Tools for carving reliefs in wood are mostly the specialized long and short-bend gouges and the firmer chisel.

The stop-cut technique is very important in relief carving in wood because the sculptor is able to score the wood to the desired depth and then, with a chisel or gouge, to make a cut that stops at the scored line. This helps to create the firm edges and outlines that are very important in creating the lapping planes that give the illusion of depth and distance.

The wooden mallet used for carving relief in wood can be lighter than the heavy one used for carving in the round. The aims of relief sculpture—to portray depth and roundness with very shallow penetrations into the wood surface—do not require heavy mallet blows.

sculpting in relief I had never met a sculptor who carved almost entirely in relief until I met Margaret Randall. The following are some of her personal observations on the subject that have evolved from her highly developed expertise in relief carving.

Relief carving is closely related to drawing. Many of the methods of creating illusions of space are similar. However, relief carving differs from drawing in one important way. All of the light and shade seen in a drawing are optical illusions. No matter where the light source is, the light and shade in a drawing remain constant. But in relief sculpture, the light and shade are created by a series of raised and depressed shapes, and by lapping edges. The light and shade are influenced by the position of the light source. The student of relief carving in wood or stone can gain immense insights by looking at the plentiful collections of this type of art on view at museums of art.

Relief sculpture is usually classified as either high or low relief. Bas-relief translated literally means low relief, but the term has come to be applied to any type of relief sculpture.

Some of the finest and best-known examples of relief sculpture are works by the ancient Egyptians, in both wood and stone. The Egyptians used relief in a very painterly fashion. Much of the depth was created by very shallow depressions; sometimes these depressions were not much more than an incised line. Yet, the illusion of space and multiple forms was completely conveyed.

The period of art known as the Renaissance, which began in Italy about the fourteenth century, introduced the use of the art of perspective in relief carving. Perspective was the major innovator which provided the artist with the ability to create the impression of great depth of space upon a totally flat plane. The illusion of real and believable space was the main concern of the Renaissance period, and with the application of perspective into relief sculpture, a greater feeling of three dimensions was introduced into the art of relief carving.

A very important point to observe in carving a relief is that the stone or wood being carved must be placed in the same position while it is being carved as it will be seen when completed. If the work is carved face up upon the work table, then stood upright to be viewed, the light and shade that may have worked well when the piece lay face up, will be contrary when the same sculpture is viewed in an upright position.

The sculptor working in relief on stone has to be much more direct than the woodcarver, because oversights made in stone are not as easily remedied as in wood. Mistakes made in wood can be corrected by gluing new slabs of wood over the injured area. The new slabs can be glued in place after sufficient preparation, such as sanding, to ensure close-fitting surfaces. Bear in mind, however, that additions may not match color and grain of the main body of the work. Therefore, staining is usually necessary whenever much patching and adding are done.

The carving process of relief sculpture is similar to that of carving in the round. The highest points of the design are the starting points; then the work moves inward toward the lower and finally lowest depths of the work. It is important to know how deep the lowest planes of the sculpture are to be, and what means will be used to communicate the illusion of depth, whether by the use of scale, overlapping planes, perspective, or by incised lines similar to drawing in concept.

The above prerequisites or necessary preconcepts are the substance which make a drawing of the proposed work indispensable to the success of the piece, because many of the design and depth problems can be worked out in the drawing. To do this, draw the image directly on the surface of the wood or stone (after proving it on paper). Use chalk, charcoal, or pencil.

My own relief carvings are done on wood; therefore, the following relates to my approach to carving relief on wood. When the final drawing of the relief-carving project is sketched out on wood, trace the outlines with a parting tool. This is a V-shaped chisel (see Figure 12–2). After outlining, proceed to block out the work by carving downward from the highest to lower points. Hold the lowest planes for the last stages. The fixing of high points in relief sculpture is quite unlike the high points of sculpture in the round. In relief sculpture, the high points are created by the sculptor to suit the design preferred.

A short-bend gouge is the best type of tool for use as a wood remover in relief sculpture. This gouge can make short scoops without disturbing or splintering the wood in surrounding areas.

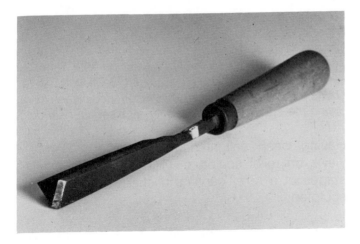

FIGURE 12–2 Parting tool. This tool is useful in making clean edges in the early stages of relief sculpture in wood. Note the V-shaped cutting edge. (Photo by Chee Heng Yeong)

Although there are no rules governing procedure preference, I find that it is better if the work is developed in a general overall fashion, rather than piece by piece. The general overall development of the work enables the sculptor to maintain control throughout the work, and to make adjustments as they are needed.

The sizes of the tools used vary with the size of the sculpture, which influences the amount of wood to be removed. Better to remove a little, and then some more, rather than to remove too much at once. As the forms are developed by the subtraction process, which creates the definitive lines and levels and planes, keep in mind the source from which the forms are derivative. Always refer to the drawings which were first done on paper.

In relief sculpture, line is defined by shadow. Shadow is created when light fails to illuminate some areas. The areas which create shadow are areas which turn sharply away from the illuminated planes. This simple concept holds the key to understanding the means with which to portray an idea in relief sculpture; accept and deny light in such a way as to define the images which make up the total design. As has been stated earlier, keep the main light source at the top. It is not possible to fix the carved definitions to accommodate diverse light sources.

To finish a work, parting tools for firming up edges, firmer chisels, scrapers and sandpaper can be used for smoothing surfaces. Keep incisions and edges sharp and clean. To ensure this, tools must be kept very well keened. Sandpaper should be used cautiously, so as not to change the planes. It is often necessary to re-define the contours and lines with a chisel after sanding.

Having been enlightened by Margaret Randall's views on relief sculpture, I'll now discuss the five stages of a relief carving in cherry wood that she sculpted.

Figure 12–3 shows the first step—a drawing of the idea upon the wood, after many preliminary drawings were made on paper. As we can see in the light and shaded areas in the drawing, the circular shape enclosing the standing figure is to be on a higher plane than the figure it encircles. This is indicated by the dark shadings around the figure. Shaded areas in a drawing indicate shadow, and

FIGURE 12–3 The departure from the relative proportions of the two major figures in the work immediately gives the sculpture its surreal, dreamlike quality. (Photo by Gil McMillon)

shadow in a relief sculpture means low or depressed areas denying the light. With this in mind, a clue is given in the drawing as to which parts of the wood are to be elevated and which parts are to be depressed. The bird in the drawing is clearly raised, and so are the twigs and berries in the upper right corner. It appears in the drawing that the sculptor intends to place the bird, the twigs, and the berries at the uppermost elevation in the scheme.

Very noticeable in Figure 12–3 is the fact that the artist has ignored scale in this composition, or rather, the artist has deliberately used two different scales in order to produce a certain mood. The bird and its surrounding berries and leaves are of a different scale than the standing figure. The familiar image of the human figure and the equally familiar form of the bird are not placed in relative proportion to each other. This departure from the relative proportions of the two major figures in the work immediately gives the sculpture its surreal, dreamlike quality, which was exactly the artist's intention.

In Figure 12–4, we see the relief sculpture in the second stage. With short-bend gouges, Margaret Randall has begun to depress the low parts of the sculpture while at the same time outlining some of the edges with a parting tool.

Relief carving, like all of the carving arts, is strictly an art of subtracting. To raise any plane of the wood's surface to a higher level, the sculptor must depress the surrounding areas until the elevated plane is as dominant as it is intended to be. Since the bird's wing and the berries and twigs are the highest planes in the sculpture, Margaret Randall began the work by carving down and in from the highest planes to the heart-shaped oval that encircles the standing figure. Some of the charcoal lines are still visible in the uncarved portions of Figure 12–4, proving such areas to be the higher planes of the sculpture. The groove that has started to

FIGURE 12–4 Some of the charcoal lines are still visible in the uncarved portions of the sculpture, proving such areas to be the higher planes. (Photo by Gil McMillon)

partially outline the heart-shaped oval was made by a parting tool. Drooping from the twig that is held in the bird's beak is a pine cone, an excellent subject for relief sculpture.

In Figure 12–5, the pine cone has disappeared. The constant disappearance and re-emergence of forms are some of the magic of carving. The beginner is naturally too timid to remove a form. The need to do this is that the forms cannot relate to each other on the same plane; therefore, in order to move the masses to different levels, the images must be erased in order to facilitate the chiseling away of excess material.

One of the preliminary drawings made on paper can be used as a reference, or drawing references can be dispensed with and the work can dictate its own independent direction as the sculptor reacts to

FIGURE 12–5 The pine cone has disappeared. The constant disappearance and re-emergence of forms is some of the magic of carving. (Photo by Gil McMillon)

the work in progress. Parts that were originally planned to be the highest planes can be changed if visual observation dictates it.

In Figure 12–5, the only planes that represent the original surface of the wood are the bird's wing and feet and the twig with pine cone. All else has been depressed at levels varying from ½ inch to 1 inch. The strong black shadow at the left is at about 1 inch in depth. The deeper the cut, the stronger the shadow.

Relief sculpture is not unlike music in its structure. If heavy chords are desired, then contrasts in light and shade are encouraged by deep undercuts and sharply turned edges, but if a more even temper is preferred, then the lights and shadows are kept more equal, with gentle undercuts prevailing. Notice the variety of gouge marks on the surface of the wood, indicating the use of more than one size and type of gouge. The broader gouge marks at the extreme left in Figure 12–5 were made by a ¾-inch short-bend gouge, but the narrow, sharp incisions at the extended arm of the figure were made by a ¼-inch short-bend gouge.

Tools are used in variety to suit the need, and the need is usually discovered rather than anticipated, because wood grains are not totally predictable.

In Figure 12–6, the forms seemingly lost in the flurry of carving are now being reclaimed. The redefining of the forms can be a moment of great anxiety for the sculptor. Decisions must be made, and the new decisions cannot always conform to

FIGURE 12–6 Notice that the berries and leaves at the top far right still maintain the original charcoal markings of the drawing, which, in the final stages, made these areas the highest points of the sculpture. (Photo by Gil McMillon)

FIGURE 12–7 The finished relief sculpture by Margaret Randall. (Photo by Gordon Cruz)

the original drawing because the penetration into the depths of the wood changes the original space relationships. Notice that the berries and leaves at the top far right still maintain the original charcoal markings of the drawing, which, in the final stages, made these areas the highest points of the sculpture (see Figure 12–7).

conclusion

It was when I found some notes that I'd made in 1966 on how to carve in wood and stone that I was reminded that from my earliest exploits into the discovery of sculpture by carving, I wanted to share the experience. I hope I have done so in such a way that you will want to try it.

The art of producing sculpture through the process of subtraction by carving is still a unique art form, one which rewards those artists willing to take the time to discover the very special secrets of anything that is unique.

The learning process is always a painful one. The expression "have fun while you learn" is partly true. Learning can be a lot of fun, but it is also a lot of hard work. Gratification comes from the result of this hard work.

index